Another Taste of Aloha

A New Collection
of Recipes
From
The Junior League of Honolulu

Serving Hawai'i's community with Aloha since 1923.

The Junior League of Honolulu, Inc. is an organization of women committed to promoting voluntarism and to improving the community through the effective action and leadership of trained volunteers. Its purpose is exclusively educational and charitable.

The Junior League of Honolulu, Inc., reaches out to women of all races, religions and national origins who demonstrate an interest in and commitment to voluntarism.

First Printing   September, 1993
Second Printing   August, 1994
Third Printing   June, 1996
Fourth Printing   August, 1998

The Junior League of Honolulu, Inc.
Commercial Publications
1050 Ala Moana Blvd., Bldg. A, Bay 1
Honolulu, Hawai'i 96814
Phone (808) 596-2006
Fax (808) 596-0206

Foreword

Nearly a decade has passed since the Junior League of Honolulu, Inc. first published "A Taste of Aloha" with its distinctive cover by noted Island artist Pegge Hopper. Those 10 years have brought change.

Many of the recipes from that first cookbook are classics. Some took a great deal of time and effort to prepare. Others relied on rich quantities of butter, cream and eggs. While we still enjoy those dishes, we find ourselves trying to do more with less: less time, less cholesterol, less fat. "Another Taste of Aloha" reflects this shift.

But the purpose of the Junior League of Honolulu, Inc. remains the same. We are still a group of women dedicated to training volunteers who will intelligently make a difference in our community. Our range of projects demonstrates the diverse concerns of our members.

From that early start in 1923, providing baby clothes to earthquake victims in Japan, projects have included planning for the restoration of Iolani Palace in the 1960s and assisting with Hale Kipa, a shelter for young runaways, in the 1970s.

The 1980s brought the Hawai'i Children's Museum, the AIDS Education comic book and the Enhancements program working with the Children's Advocacy Center of Honolulu to help young victims of sexual abuse.

The years ahead promise a continuing focus on social issues, especially as they affect the family. In welcoming you to our new book, we are proud to continue our association with the talented Pegge Hopper.

The glossary at the back of the book provides additional information about ingredients or terms marked with an asterisk(*).

We hope you will consider "Another Taste of Aloha" as a companion to our first volume in your kitchen library, another celebration of our unique Island culture.

Hana hou!

*This book is made possible in part
through the generous financial support of
Bank of Hawaii
and
Cooke Foundation, Limited*

Table of Contents

Introduction

Aloha. A gentle word, it is the heart of Hawai'i. *Aloha* stands not only for love among the people of this land, but for a love of the land itself. The two are inseparable.

The early Hawaiians lived in harmony and with respect for the land, the sea and all of nature. The land was their life, and its preservation meant the preservation of their people. This remains true today.

The concept of *ohana*, or family, has from the beginning been understood by the Hawaiians better than by most peoples of the world. Also important to their way of life were the concepts of *kokua*, meaning help and cooperation, and *ho'oponopono*, which was the just and peaceful settlement of disputes through community arbitration.

Hawai'i remains one of the few places on earth where so many ethnic groups co-exist in harmony. Hawaiians, Caucasians, Chinese, Japanese, Filipino, Portuguese, Korean and more have developed a respect for each other and the customs they brought here. This has created, not so much a melting pot where distinctions disappear, but a rich and wholesome stew.

The individual ingredients are still clearly recognizable, but together they have produced a unique blend where each enhances the others. In celebrating our differences, we remember to keep our separate identities alive.

Hawai'i's people have preserved their cultures and customs. Here we celebrate Christmas and the Fourth of July, but we also observe the traditions of Chinese New Year with lion dances and firecrackers. We anticipate the summer *bon* dances and the launching of tiny paper boats into the sea in memory of the departed in the Japanese tradition.

Hawaiians commemorate Kamehameha the Great with a parade of floats decorated with thousands of fresh flowers and King Kalakaua is remembered with the delightful Merrie Monarch Hula Festival. The *ukulele*, brought here by the Portuguese, has become synonymous with Hawaiian music.

Here we live with influences from all the cultures that have arrived in Hawai'i because all of us are immigrants. This has certainly affected the way we eat.

The *lu'au* is the oldest and only indigenous celebration in Hawai'i. Important events were celebrated at a great feast of pork and fish, *taro* and coconut. Today, a *lu'au* celebration to mark a baby's first birthday may typically include such Hawaiian specialties as *laulau* and *kalua* pig, but also look for Japanese *sashimi* of raw tuna, spicy Korean *taegu*, and platters of Chinese noodles and Filipino pork *adobo*.

You will find hard-working volunteers at school or church carnival booths frying a Portuguese doughnut called a *malasada* and broiling meat soaked in soy sauce and threaded on sticks. Vietnamese shrimp rolls, introduced by our most recent settlers from Southeast Asia, are fast becoming a staple of outdoor dinners, and Thai restaurants thrive all over the state.

Saimin, a local adaptation of Japanese *ramen,* is a noodle and broth treat that is so popular that it is on a local menu of a major national fast-food chain.

The people who live here are eager to share their homeland specialties and to sample the favorites from other cultures. Tailgate picnics at football games and diplomatic receptions at Washington Place, the residence of Hawai'i's governors, are as likely to feature *sushi* and Chinese egg rolls as hot dogs or finger sandwiches.

People from many ethnic backgrounds make up the wonder that is Hawai'i. We have come together to create our own place on earth, flavored by the diverse cultures who together share *aloha.*

Robbie Dingeman
Mary Mau
Lois Taylor

9

Children in Hawai'i are much cherished by the many cultures who come together here. A baby's first birthday is traditionally a time to throw a big luau or party for all to cheer the young life.

Appetizers and Pupus

Lemon Marinated Shrimp   *Serves 6*

2 pounds	medium shrimp, cooked and deveined
1	lemon, thinly sliced
1	onion, thinly sliced
1 (6-ounce) can	pitted black olives (optional)

Marinade

½ cup	lemon juice
1 tablespoon	white wine vinegar*
¼ cup	vegetable oil
1 clove	garlic, minced
½	bay leaf
1 teaspoon	dry mustard
1 teaspoon	salt
⅛ teaspoon	cayenne

Combine shrimp, lemon, onion and olives. Mix the marinade ingredients together and pour over shrimp. Cover and refrigerate for at least 6 hours.

To devein shrimp, make a shallow cut lengthwise down the back of each shrimp and rinse with water. Cook shrimp in boiling salted water until they are pink. Rinse under cold water to stop the cooking process.

Hawaiian Scallop Seviche   *Serves 8*

1½ pounds	jumbo scallops
1¼ cups	fresh lime juice
1 (4-ounce) can	diced green chilies, undrained
1 cup	Maui onion,* minced
1 teaspoon	salt
½ teaspoon	oregano
¼ cup	olive oil*
2 large	tomatoes, peeled, seeded and chopped
Garnish:	*Lettuce leaves, avocado slices, chopped parsley and chopped green onion*

Cut scallops into ½-inch pieces. Marinate in lime juice for 3 hours or overnight. Refrigerate, stirring frequently. Combine scallops and lime juice with remaining ingredients. Using a slotted spoon, place scallops into serving bowl lined with lettuce and garnish with avocado slices, parsley and green onions.

Layered Caviar Mold

Serves 10 – 12

1 package	unflavored gelatin
¼ cup	cold water
4	hard-cooked eggs, chopped
8 tablespoons	mayonnaise
¼ cup	fresh parsley, chopped
2	green onions, chopped
dash	hot pepper sauce
	salt and freshly ground
	white pepper to taste
1	avocado, pureed
1	avocado, diced
2 tablespoons	Maui onion,* minced
2 tablespoons	fresh lemon juice
¼ teaspoon	hot pepper sauce*
	freshly ground black pepper to taste
1 cup	sour cream
¼ cup	Maui onion,* minced
4 ounces	black caviar
1 – 1½ loaves	pumpernickel bread, thinly sliced

Line the bottom of a 9-inch springform pan with foil. Lightly oil bottom and sides. Soften gelatin in the water. Heat to liquefy. Combine eggs, 6 tablespoons mayonnaise, parsley, green onions, hot pepper sauce, salt and white pepper. Add 1 tablespoon of the gelatin and fold together gently. Spread into the springform pan and smooth the top. Combine the avocados, 2 tablespoons onion, lemon juice, the remaining 2 tablespoons mayonnaise, hot pepper sauce, salt and black pepper with 1 tablespoon of the gelatin. Gently spread over the egg mixture

continued...

and smooth the top. Mix the sour cream and remaining 2 tablespoons onion with the remaining gelatin. Spread over the avocado layer. Cover and refrigerate overnight. When ready to serve, remove sides from the springform pan and place mold on serving platter. Spread caviar over the top. Serve with the pumpernickel bread.

Hot Artichoke and Spinach Dip

Serves 6– 8

1 cup	**Parmesan cheese,* grated**
1 cup	**mayonnaise**
1 (10-ounce) package	**frozen spinach, thawed and drained**
1 (6-ounce) jar	**marinated artichoke hearts, drained and chopped**
1 (7-ounce) can	**green chilies, drained and chopped**
½ teaspoon	**crushed red pepper**
1 (2-ounce) jar	**pimento, chopped**

Mix the cheese with the mayonnaise until well blended. Add the spinach, artichoke hearts, and green chilies to the mixture and blend well. Spread mixture into 8-inch round cake pan or divide into 2 oven-proof bowls. Sprinkle red pepper and chopped pimento over top. Broil for 10 to 15 minutes or until brown and dip is hot. Serve with crackers.

Shrimp Maunakea*

Serves 8

*The blend of colors and flavors is reminiscent of Chinatown's
Maunakea Street.*

20	**large shrimp, cooked and deveined**
1 small bunch	**mint**
1 small bunch	**basil**
1 small bunch	**Chinese parsley***
20	**snow peas,* blanched**

Wrap each shrimp with a basil leaf, mint leaf, a sprig of
Chinese parsley and a snow pea. Then, skewer on a toothpick.
Serve at room temperature with Peanut Dip.

Peanut Dip

3 tablespoons	**chunky peanut butter**
¼ cup	**soy sauce***
3 tablespoons	**vinegar**
1 tablespoon	**sugar**
2 teaspoons	**fresh lime juice**
1	**chili pepper, mashed**
1 clove	**garlic, finely minced**

Combine all ingredients in microwave-safe bowl. Heat on
HIGH for 30 seconds and stir to blend.
Note: This may be made ahead. Cover and refrigerate.
Reheat before serving.

Shrimp Maunakea was first published in **My Best Recipe: Winning
Recipes** *from The Honolulu Advertiser. Used with permission of The
Bess Press, Inc.*

Asian Fish Salad

Serves 12

1 pound	fresh fish fillets, a'u* or nairagi*
1/2 cup	green onion, diced
1 cup	Chinese parsley,* minced
1/2 cup	pickled scallions,* sliced
1/4 cup	vegetable oil
4 teaspoons	ginger,* freshly grated
1/4 cup	soy sauce*

Cut fish fillets across the grain in 2-inch by 1-inch slices and about 1/4-inch thick. Arrange slices on serving platter in one layer. Top with green onion, Chinese parsley, and pickled scallions. Heat oil in saucepan until it begins to smoke, then remove pan from stove and let cool to room temperature. Pour oil over fish. Serve with grated fresh ginger mixed with soy sauce as a dipping sauce.

Cheesy Crab Dip

Makes 6 cups

2 cups	Cheddar cheese, grated
1 1/2 cups	mayonnaise
2 cups	imitation crab meat
1/2	medium onion, chopped
1 clove	garlic, chopped

Preheat oven to 350 degrees. Combine ingredients and bake for 30 minutes. Serve warm with assorted crackers or carrot sticks.

Cranberry-Glazed Brie

Serves 12

Cranberry Glaze

1 (12-ounce) bag	cranberries (if using canned delete ⅓ cup water)
¼ cup	light brown sugar
⅓ cup	dried currants
⅓ cup	water
⅛ teaspoon	dry mustard
⅛ teaspoon	ground allspice
⅛ teaspoon	ground cardamom
⅛ teaspoon	ground cloves
⅛ teaspoon	ground ginger

Combine all ingredients in heavy non-aluminum saucepan. Cook over medium-high heat until most of berries pop, stirring frequently, about 5 minutes. Cool to room temperature. Cover and refrigerate for up to 3 days or until ready to serve.

1 2.2-pound	Brie cheese wheel (8-inch diameter)
	Crackers
	Apple slices
	Pear slices

Preheat oven to 300 degrees. Using a sharp knife, cut circle in center of top rind of cheese, leaving ½-inch border of rind. Carefully remove circle of rind from cheese. Do not cut through side rind. Place cheese in 8-inch diameter ceramic baking dish or on cookie sheet lined with foil. Spread cranberry glaze on top. (Note: This may be prepared up to 6 hours ahead. Cover and refrigerate. Bring cheese to room temperature before continuing.) Bake cheese until soft, about 12 minutes. Set cheese on large platter. Surround with crackers and fruit. Cool slightly. Serve warm or at room temperature.

Macadamia Nut
Cheese Balls

Serves 10

12 ounces	cream cheese, softened
4 ounces	crushed pineapple,* thoroughly drained
¼ cup	Maui onion,* finely chopped
1 ounce	pimento, diced and drained
1 teaspoon	seasoned salt
⅓ cup	macadamia nuts* or pecans, finely chopped
Garnish:	*Parsley*

Combine cream cheese, pineapple, onion, pimento, and seasoned salt. Chill until mixture can be formed into a ball. Remove and shape into 2 or 3 balls. Roll in nuts and garnish with parsley. Serve with assorted crackers or wafers.

Indian Chutney Dip

Serves 6 – 8

8 ounces	cream cheese, softened
2 teaspoons	curry powder
¾ cup	unsalted peanuts, chopped
6	green onions, chopped
8 ounces	Bengal hot chutney or mango chutney*

Blend cream cheese, curry powder, peanuts and green onions. Chill for 6 hours or overnight to enhance flavor. Pour chutney over cream cheese mixture and serve with melba toast or mild crackers.

Leeks and Ham

Serves 4

4   **leeks,* cleaned and blanched**
4 slices   **Black Forest ham, thinly sliced**
½ cup   **Parmesan cheese,* grated**

Preheat oven to 375 degrees. Wrap each leek in a slice of ham and place in a shallow baking dish. Sprinkle top with Parmesan cheese and bake until cheese is melted and ham is crisp, about 30 minutes.

Spiced Pecans

Serves 10

2 cups   **pecan halves**
1   **egg white**
1 teaspoon   **water**
¾ cup   **sugar**
1 teaspoon   **salt**
1½ teaspoons   **cinnamon**
½ teaspoon   **ground cloves**
½ teaspoon   **nutmeg**

Preheat oven to 275 degrees. Beat egg white lightly with water. Combine sugar, salt, and spices. Dip pecans in egg whites and roll in sugar mixture. Place on buttered cookie sheet. Bake for 30 minutes. Remove pecans from cookie sheet while they are still warm or sugar will caramelize and nuts will stick together.

Dilled Carrots

Serves 8

2 pounds	carrots, julienned and blanched
2 teaspoons	dried dill weed
2 teaspoons	mustard seed
4 cloves	garlic, halved
1¼ cups	water
½ cup	cider vinegar
¼ cup	sugar

Place carrots in a bowl. Sprinkle with dill weed, mustard seed, and garlic. In a saucepan, combine water, vinegar, sugar and bring to a boil. Pour over carrots. Cool. Cover and chill overnight. Remove garlic before serving.

Note: This may be stored in the refrigerator for 2 weeks.

Pali Picante Sauce

Makes 2 cups

1 (16-ounce) can	Mexican-style stewed tomatoes, coarsely chopped
½ medium	onion, minced
2 tablespoons	Chinese parsley,* chopped

Combine ingredients. Cover and chill 1 hour. Serve with tortilla or corn chips.

Shrimp Artichoke Dip

Serves 6

2 (14-ounce) cans	artichoke hearts, drained and chopped
2 cups	mayonnaise
2 cups	Parmesan cheese,* grated
6 ounces	tiny shrimp, cooked
2 teaspoons	butter or margarine
½ cup	bread crumbs

Preheat oven to 325 degrees. Combine artichokes, mayonnaise, and cheese, mixing well. Gently stir in shrimp. Spoon into a lightly greased 1½-quart casserole dish. Melt butter or margarine in skillet. Add dried bread crumbs and stir until browned. Top artichoke and shrimp mixture with bread crumbs. Bake for 15 to 20 minutes. Serve with table water crackers.

Variation: To make Seafood Artichoke Dip, substitute 6 ounces of cooked crabmeat for the shrimp.

Herb Dip

1 cup	mayonnaise
¼ cup	sour cream
¼ cup	plain yogurt
½ teaspoon	chives
½ teaspoon	thyme
pinch	salt
½ – 1 teaspoon	curry powder
1 tablespoon	parsley
1 tablespoon	onion, grated
1½ teaspoons	lemon juice
½ teaspoon	Worcestershire sauce
	assorted vegetables

Combine ingredients and chill for 4 hours. Serve with assorted vegetables.

Note: This may be thinned with a touch of buttermilk and used as a salad dressing.

Blackened Ahi
in Butter Sauce

2 tablespoons	dry mustard
1 tablespoon	water
3 tablespoons	soy sauce*
½ cup	white wine
⅛ cup	white wine vinegar*
⅓ cup	onion, chopped
2 ounces	heavy cream
½ cup	butter
dash	freshly ground pepper
1 teaspoon	olive oil*
2 (½-pound) blocks	ahi*
	olive oil*
	Cajun seasoning*
	black sesame seeds*
Garnish:	*Parsley*

Mix mustard, water and soy sauce in small bowl until smooth. Set aside. In small saucepan over medium heat, combine wine, vinegar and onion. Cook until about 3 tablespoons of liquid remain, about 15-20 minutes. Add cream and bring to a boil. Add butter and stir until melted. Stir in mustard-soy sauce mixture and pepper. Set aside. Put 1 teaspoon of olive oil in a heavy skillet and heat on high until very hot. Cut fish fillets in 2-inch by 6-inch slices, about 1-inch thick. Rub remaining olive oil on fish slices. Sprinkle heavily with Cajun seasoning. Sear fish in oil for 5 seconds on each of the 4 sides (fish should be raw in the middle). Cut fish across the grain in ¼-inch thick slices. Cover surface of serving platter with marinade. Arrange fish slices in an overlapping pattern on top of marinade and sprinkle with sesame seeds. Garnish with parsley and serve.

Jessica's Salsa

Makes 4 cups

2 (14.5-ounce) cans	Mexican-style stewed tomatoes, coarsely chopped
½ cup	Chinese parsley,* stemmed and chopped
2 – 3 cloves	garlic, minced
1	small Maui onion,* chopped
1	small lime, juiced
½ teaspoon	salt
2	jalapeno peppers, seeded, cored, and chopped

Combine all ingredients. Cover and chill for at least 1 hour. Serve with tortilla or corn chips. For hotter salsa, add more peppers.

Bruschette

Serves 8

2	Kula or Kahuku tomatoes,* seeded, juiced and chopped
1 clove	garlic, chopped
1 teaspoon	green onion, finely chopped
1 teaspoon	first pressed olive oil*
2 tablespoons	fresh basil, chopped
8 pieces	sourdough bread rounds
½ cup	mozzarella cheese, grated

Combine tomatoes, garlic, green onion, olive oil and basil. Sprinkle bread rounds with mozzarella and toast under broiler until cheese is melted and light golden brown. Remove from oven and top with tomato mixture. Serve immediately.

Sunset Seviche

Serves 6 – 8

1 pound	sole fillets or 'opakapaka*
8 tablespoons	fresh lime juice
1 large	avocado
1 large	tomato, peeled, seeded and coarsely chopped
8 – 10	green onions, including tops, finely sliced
1 tablespoon	fresh Chinese parsley,* minced
1½ teaspoons	salt
Dash	freshly ground pepper
1 clove	garlic, minced
	lettuce leaves

Cut fish across the grain into ½-inch cubes. Marinate in lime juice for at least 4 hours. Refrigerate, stirring frequently. The fish should lose its translucent appearance. One hour before serving, mash the avocado in a medium-sized mixing bowl. Add tomato, green onions, Chinese parsley, salt, pepper, and garlic. Drain the fish and add to the avocado mixture. Refrigerate until ready to serve. Serve on a bed of lettuce leaves.

Brie with Sun-Dried Tomato Topping

Serves 16

1 pound	Brie cheese
3 tablespoons	parsley, minced
3 tablespoons	Parmesan cheese,* grated
5	sun-dried tomatoes, packed in oil, minced and drained
1 tablespoon	oil, from sun-dried tomatoes
3 cloves	garlic, minced
1 tablespoon	fresh basil, minced
1½ tablespoons	toasted pine nuts, coarsely chopped
¼ cup	fresh tomatoes, chopped

Chill Brie well before handling. Remove rind from top and place cheese on serving platter. Combine remaining ingredients and spread on top of Brie. For optimum flavor, allow cheese to stand for 30 – 60 minutes at room temperature before serving.

Note: This may be prepared up to 6 hours ahead. Cover and refrigerate. Bring cheese to room temperature before serving.

Thai Lettuce Rolls

Serves 3 – 4

7 – 8 leaves	Manoa,* or butter lettuce
5 – 6 slices	cucumber, seeded
4 (½-inch) cubes	firm tofu,* drained
4 (¼-inch) strips	red bell pepper
4 (¼-inch) strips	green bell pepper
4 (¼-inch) strips	yellow bell pepper
2 tablespoons	bean sprouts*
5 – 6 leaves	mint
5 – 6 leaves	basil
2 sprigs	Chinese parsley*
	kampyo* (see note)
	peanuts, finely chopped

Dressing

⅓ cup	lime juice
6 ounces	fish sauce*
1 stalk	(bottom part only) lemon grass,* sliced thin, crosswise
2	serrano chilies, finely diced
3 cups	water
¾ cup	sugar
1 teaspoon	dried red chili, crushed

Combine dressing ingredients and stir until sugar is dissolved. Let stand one day before serving. Top dressing with peanuts immediately before serving. Lay 3 or 4 leaves of lettuce with edges slightly overlapping on a plate. Layer half of cucumber, tofu, peppers, bean sprouts, mint and basil on lettuce. Roll lettuce to create a bun, leaving ends open. Tie with

continued...

kampyo. Repeat. Place two lettuce rolls on a plate. Garnish with Chinese parsley. Serve with dressing on the side for dipping.

Note: Dried kampyo may be simmered in equal parts of water and chicken stock until tender.

Salmon Ball

Makes 2 cups

1 (7¾-ounce) can	salmon, drained
6 ounces	cream cheese, softened
1 tablespoon	lemon juice
2 teaspoons	onion, grated
1 teaspoon	prepared horseradish
¼ teaspoon	salt
½ teaspoon	liquid smoke
⅓ cup	walnuts, chopped
3 tablespoons	parsley, chopped

Combine salmon, cream cheese, lemon juice, onion, horseradish, salt and liquid smoke. Blend thoroughly. Chill for 6 hours or overnight to enhance flavor. Mix walnuts and parsley. Form salmon mixture into a ball and roll in the walnut-parsley mixture. Serve with wheat crackers.

Avocado and Shrimp Salad

4	**lettuce leaves**
1	**avocado, thinly sliced**
½ cup	**sour cream**
5¼ ounces	**cream cheese, softened**
3 teaspoons	**lumpfish roe or caviar**
1½ teaspoons	**dill**
12	**large shrimp, cooked, shelled, and deveined**

Place lettuce leaves on serving plates. Divide the avocado slices equally between the serving plates, arranging the slices in a fan shape. Mix the sour cream, cream cheese, roe and dill and pour over the avocados. Top with shrimp and serve immediately.

Island Curry Layers

8 ounces	**cream cheese, softened**
1 cup	**cottage cheese**
¼ cup	**sour cream**
2 teaspoons	**curry powder**
1 cup	**Indian-style chutney***
⅓ cup	**green onions, chopped**
⅓ cup	**raisins, chopped**
⅓ cup	**coconut,* shredded**
1 cup	**cooked chicken, chopped**
½ cup	**salted peanuts, chopped**

Combine cream cheese, cottage cheese, sour cream, and curry powder, blending until smooth. Spread into serving dish. Top with chutney, green onions, raisins, coconut, chicken and peanuts. Cover and chill for 4 hours or overnight to blend flavors. Serve with assorted crackers.

Stuffed Snow Peas

Makes 100 pieces

4 ounces	**crab meat, finely chopped**
3	**green onions, chopped**
⅓ teaspoon	**dill**
	juice of ½ lemon
2 tablespoons	**sour cream**
	salt and freshly ground pepper
	to taste
100	**snow peas***
Garnish:	*Parsley*

Combine crab meat, green onion, dill, lemon juice, sour cream, salt and pepper, blending until smooth. Remove stem end from snow peas, string them, and blanch in boiling water for 30 seconds. Drain and immerse in ice water. Drain again. With a small sharp knife, slit open the straight seam of each snow pea and stuff crab-sour cream mixture into each one, using a small spoon, butter knife or a pastry bag. Garnish and serve.

Tutu's Chicken Delight

Serves 6

Tutu is the Hawaiian nickname for grandmother.

3½ pounds	**drummettes**
	salt
½ – ¾ cup	**cornstarch**
	vegetable oil
2 cups	**water**
2 cups	**soy sauce***
¾ cup	**brown sugar**
3 tablespoons	**sesame oil***
3 tablespoons	**sesame seeds***
3	**green onions, finely chopped**
Garnish:	*Sesame seeds* and chopped green onions*

Lightly salt drummettes and roll in cornstarch. Stir fry in oil until light brown. Drain. Combine water, soy sauce, brown sugar, sesame oil, sesame seeds and green onions in a shallow pan. Marinate drummettes in mixture for 1 hour at room temperature. Drain and broil until brown and crispy, about 10 minutes per side. Sprinkle with sesame seeds and chopped green onions. Serve hot or cold.

Family and friends leave their shoes and slippers
at the front door when they enter most Island homes.
The no-shoe tradition is now almost universal.

Beverages

Waikiki Workout

Serves 1

8 ounces	orange juice
1	banana
1	kiwi fruit
1 tablespoon	honey
	ice

Pour juice in blender. Add banana, kiwi and honey and blend until smooth. Add ice and blend until thick. Serve.

Tropical Fruit Cooler

Makes 1½ gallons

6 cups	water
4 cups	sugar
1 (48-ounce) can	pineapple* juice
6	bananas
1 (6-ounce) can	frozen orange juice concentrate, thawed
½ cup	fresh lemon juice
1 gallon	ginger ale
½ gallon	club soda
Garnish:	*Orange slices and lemon slices*

Boil sugar in water to dissolve. Let cool. Blend juices and bananas in a blender. Mix with sugar and water syrup and freeze in two blocks. Thirty to forty-five minutes before serving, pour half ginger ale over frozen mixture in punch bowl. Add remaining ginger ale and club soda. Garnish and serve.

Pineapple Plantation Punch

Serves 1

1 ounce	light rum
½ ounce	dark rum
3 ounces	freshly squeezed orange juice
2 ounces	pineapple* juice
	splash of grenadine
¼ cup	sweet and sour mix
	squeeze of lemon
Garnish:	Orange wedge, lemon wedge and a cherry

Mix all ingredients together. Serve over crushed ice in a tall glass. Garnish with orange and lemon wedges and a cherry.

Rosemary Lemonade

Makes 1 gallon

8 cups	water
3 cups	fresh lemon juice (about 7-8 large lemons)
1½ cups	sugar
2 teaspoons	crushed fresh rosemary
Garnish:	Fresh rosemary

Combine water, lemon juice and sugar in a large non-aluminum pot. Bring to a boil, stirring occasionally. Remove from heat and stir in rosemary. Let stand 10 minutes. Discard rosemary. Strain and chill. Garnish with fresh rosemary.

Lana'i Fizz

Makes 1 gallon

1 (12-ounce) can	frozen orange juice concentrate, thawed
1 (12-ounce) can	frozen pineapple* juice concentrate, thawed
¼ cup	lemon juice
2 bottles	champagne, chilled
1 liter	lemon-lime soda, chilled
Garnish:	*Orange slices*

Mix juices together and chill. Just before serving, add champagne and soda. Stir and garnish with floating orange slices.

Margarita Punch

Makes 10 – 12 cups

1 (12-ounce) can	frozen lemonade concentrate, thawed
1 (12-ounce) can	frozen limeade concentrate, thawed
½ (1.5 liter) bottle	jug white wine (preferably Chenin Blanc), chilled

Mix the ingredients together. Pour over ice and serve.

Hawaiian Cooler

Makes 8 cups

1	**lemon**
1	**orange**
2 tablespoons	**sugar**
2 cups	**pineapple* juice, chilled**
2 cups	**dry white wine, chilled**
1½ cups	**sparkling water, chilled**
Garnish:	*Mint sprigs and sliced strawberries*

Cut 2 or 3 thin slices from centers of lemon and orange. Place slices in a 2 – 3-quart pitcher. Squeeze juice from ends of fruit into the pitcher. Add sugar and pineapple juice, stirring to dissolve sugar. Stir in wine and sparkling water. Serve over ice in a punch bowl or over crushed ice in a stemmed glass. Garnish and serve.

Lilikoi
Strawberry Punch

Makes 1 gallon

1 (6-ounce) can	**frozen lemonade concentrate,** **thawed**
1 (6-ounce) can	**frozen orange juice concentrate,** **thawed**
1 (6-ounce) can	**frozen passion fruit juice** **concentrate, thawed**
3 cups	**cold water**
1 (1-liter) bottle	**ginger ale, chilled**
2 pints	**fresh strawberries, hulled and sliced**
Garnish:	*Orange slices and mint leaves*

Combine ingredients in a punchbowl and float strawberry slices on top. Garnish with orange slices and mint leaves.

Kona Coffee Punch

Makes 5 – 6 quarts

4 quarts	strong Kona coffee,* chilled
1 quart	whipping cream
5 tablespoons	sugar
5 teaspoons	vanilla
2 quarts	vanilla ice cream
4 ounces	chocolate syrup (optional)
1 cup	coffee liqueur (optional)
Garnish:	*Chocolate shavings*

Whip cream until stiff peaks form, gradually adding sugar and vanilla. Combine coffee, chocolate syrup and coffee liqueur. Spoon ice cream into a large punch bowl and carefully pour in chilled coffee mixture. Top with mounds of whipped cream. Garnish with chocolate shavings and serve.

Kona coffee is one of the most sought after origin coffees in the world. Grown on the west coast of the "Big Island" of Hawai'i, these coffee beans benefit from a unique cloud cover that appears around two o'clock every afternoon, just in time to protect the delicate trees from the intense heat of the tropical sun. Its medium body, fair acidity and wine-like tones produce a rich aroma.

Blue Hawai'i Coffee
Makes 1 pound

¼ pound	Jamaican Blue Mountain coffee beans
¼ pound	Kona coffee* beans
½ pound	Sumatra coffee beans

Mix ingredients together and store in an airtight container. This can be kept in the freezer for up to 2 months.

Honolulu Blend Coffee
Makes 1 pound

¼ pound	Kona Espresso coffee beans
¼ pound	Vienna Roast coffee beans
½ pound	Colombian Supremo coffee beans

Mix ingredients together and store in an airtight container. This can be kept in the freezer for up to 2 months.

*Is it summertime already? Or maybe
just a warm day in January. Our mild climate
means that parks and beaches are open
all year round for swimming, surfing
or just playing in the sand.*

Salads and Salad Dressings

Cold Steak Salad

Serves 8

This salad serves four as an entree.

2 pounds	boneless sirloin steak, cut about 2 inches thick
	salt and freshly ground pepper
½ pound	mushrooms, sliced
½ cup	scallions, sliced
1 (14-ounce) can	hearts of palm, drained and sliced
2 tablespoons	chives, chopped
2 tablespoons	parsley, chopped
2 teaspoons	dried dill
1 head	romaine lettuce

Dressing

1	egg (see Note)
½ cup	olive oil*
3 tablespoons	tarragon* or white wine vinegar*
4 teaspoons	Dijon mustard*
1 teaspoon	salt
2 teaspoons	lemon juice
1 teaspoon	Worcestershire sauce
dash	Tabasco
Garnish:	*2 medium tomatoes, sliced*

Season both sides of the steak with salt and pepper. Broil until medium-rare, about 8 – 10 minutes per side. Cool slightly and cut into ⅛-inch slices. Combine remaining salad ingredients and mix with steak slices. To prepare dressing, place the egg in a food processor or blender. With motor running, slowly add oil. Add remaining ingredients and blend well. Pour over steak salad and mix until well coated. Garnish. Serve cold or at room temperature.

Note: Egg substitute may be used instead of the raw egg in the dressing.

Freeze the steak slightly for ease in cutting.

"Charlie the Tuna" Salad *Serves 4 - 6*

1½ pounds	**ahi* steaks, 1¼-inches thick**
	salt and freshly ground pepper
	garlic powder
	olive oil*
½ cup	**mayonnaise**
3½ ounces	**capers***
1 tablespoon	**lemon juice**
1 teaspoon	**dill weed**

Season fish with salt, pepper and garlic powder. Brush a light coat of olive oil on each steak so that it will not stick to the grill. Grill over hot coals until no longer pink on the inside, about 10 minutes per side. Cool and chop against the grain into ¼-inch chunks. Combine mayonnaise with capers, lemon juice and dill weed and gently mix with fish. Tuna should remain in chunks. Chill before serving. Serve as a salad or with bread, crackers or chips.

Aegean Spinach Salad

Serves 4 - 6

The traditional spinach salad goes Greek.

1 pound	fresh spinach, washed, trimmed and torn in bite-size pieces
2 cloves	garlic, minced
2 tablespoons	fresh mint, finely chopped
8 – 12	Kalamata* olives
1 small	red onion, quartered and thinly sliced
2 tablespoons	red wine vinegar*
6 ounces	feta cheese,* crumbled
6 tablespoons	olive oil*
3 cups	croutons
	freshly ground pepper to taste

Put spinach in a large bowl. Add garlic, mint, olives, onion, vinegar and cheese. Heat olive oil almost to smoking. Pour over salad. Add croutons and toss quickly. Taste and season with pepper or more vinegar, if necessary. Serve immediately.

Pepper Tomato Vinaigrette

Serves 6

½ cup	**red wine vinegar***
2 – 3 tablespoons	**sugar**
2 tablespoons	**fresh lemon juice**
2 cloves	**garlic, minced**
¼ **teaspoon**	**freshly ground pepper**
½ **teaspoon**	**salt**
2 tablespoons	**fresh basil leaves, chopped**
1	**green bell pepper, thinly sliced**
1	**red bell pepper, thinly sliced (optional)**
1	**yellow bell pepper, thinly sliced (optional)**
3 – 4 medium	**tomatoes, thinly sliced**
1	**Maui onion,* thinly sliced, separated**
1	**Japanese cucumber,* thinly sliced (optional)**

Combine vinegar, sugar, lemon juice, garlic, pepper, salt and basil in a jar. Shake well. Layer pepper, tomato and onion slices in a salad bowl. Pour marinade over vegetables. Cover and chill for six hours or overnight to enhance flavor.

Curried Rice with Artichokes

Serves 6 - 8

2 cups	rice cooked in chicken stock
3 – 4	scallions, sliced thin
½	green bell pepper, seeded and chopped
12	pimento-stuffed olives, sliced
2 (6-ounce) jars	marinated artichoke hearts
¾ teaspoon	curry powder
⅓ cup	mayonnaise

Combine rice, scallions, green pepper and olives. Drain artichoke hearts, reserving the marinade. Cut artichoke hearts in half. Combine marinade with curry powder and mayonnaise. Add artichoke hearts to rice mixture and toss with the dressing. Cover and chill before serving.

Minty Lentil Salad

Serves 4 - 6

An interesting combination of flavors.

1 cup	dried lentils
1½ cups	fresh bean sprouts*
½ cup	fresh mint leaves, coarsely chopped
¼ cup	red onion, minced
¼ cup	freshly squeezed orange juice
2 tablespoons	extra virgin olive oil*
1 tablespoon	balsamic vinegar*
1 teaspoon	orange zest, minced
1 teaspoon	salt
	freshly ground pepper to taste

Bring a saucepan of lightly salted water to a boil and add lentils. Reduce the heat and simmer until crisp-tender, about 20–30 minutes. Drain, rinse under cold water and pat dry. Combine remaining ingredients and mix with lentils. Toss well to combine. Cover and chill for several hours or overnight.

Petite Potato Salad

6 – 8	new red potatoes, scrubbed and quartered
¼ cup	red wine vinegar*
⅓ cup	extra virgin olive oil*
	salt and freshly ground pepper to taste
4 ounces	Roquefort cheese, crumbled
1	yellow bell pepper, cored, seeded and cut into ½-inch cubes
¼ cup	red onion, cut into ½-inch cubes
4 strips	bacon, fried and cut into 3-inch pieces
2 tablespoons	fresh parsley, minced
Garnish:	*Chinese parsley* *

Bring a saucepan of lightly salted water to a boil and add potatoes. Boil until tender, about 7 minutes. Drain. In a small bowl, combine vinegar, oil, pepper, and salt. Pour over the potatoes and mix until well coated. Add ⅔ of the Roquefort cheese. Toss. Add yellow peppers and onion and toss. Add bacon and parsley. Top with the remaining Roquefort cheese and serve at room temperature.

Green Bean and Cauliflower Salad

Serves 6 – 8

A colorful and refreshing summer salad.

1 medium	**cauliflower, cut into florets**
¾ pound	**fresh green beans, cut into 1-inch pieces**
1 small	**red onion, thinly sliced**

Dressing

⅔ cup	**vegetable oil**
⅓ cup	**white wine vinegar***
½ teaspoon	**dry mustard**
½ teaspoon	**sugar**
1 teaspoon	**basil, crushed**
1 teaspoon	**salt**
¼ teaspoon	**freshly ground pepper**
Garnish:	*Tomato wedges and chopped hard-cooked eggs*

Cook the cauliflower florets until just tender, about 3 minutes. Rinse with cold water. Set aside. Cook the beans until tender, approximately 4 – 5 minutes. Rinse in cold water. Combine cauliflower, green beans and onion. Mix dressing ingredients and pour over the vegetables, mixing lightly. Cover and chill for 2 to 4 hours. To serve, remove the vegetables from the marinade and place on a serving platter. Garnish with tomato wedges and chopped hard-cooked eggs. Drizzle with 2 tablespoons of the marinade.

Macadamia Nut Pea Salad   *Serves 6*

1 (16-ounce) package	frozen peas
1 cup	celery, chopped
¼ cup	green onions, including 3 – 4 inches of green tops, chopped
1 cup	macadamia nuts* or cashews, chopped
¼ cup	bacon, fried crisp and crumbled
1 cup	sour cream
½ teaspoon	salt
¼ cup	Dressing
	Boston or Manoa* lettuce leaves

Dressing

1½ teaspoons	lemon juice
½ cup	red wine vinegar*
1 teaspoon	salt
½ teaspoon	freshly ground pepper
1½ teaspoons	Worcestershire sauce
½ teaspoon	Dijon mustard*
1 clove	garlic, crushed
2 tablespoons	sugar
1½ teaspoons	grated onion and juice
1½ cups	corn oil

Blend the dressing ingredients except the oil. Add oil and beat thoroughly. Store in the refrigerator if not used immediately. Turn frozen peas into a colander and rinse until thawed. Drain. Combine peas, celery, onion, nuts and bacon. Mix sour cream, salt and ¼ cup dressing and pour over salad, mixing lightly. Cover and chill, preferably overnight. Serve on a bed of lettuce. Remaining dressing may be refrigerated for later use.

Onion juice is obtained by grating a large white onion on the fine side of a grater or processing it in an electric blender and straining the puree.

Tropical Spinach Salad   *Serves 10 – 12*

1 pound	fresh spinach, washed, trimmed and torn in bite-size pieces
3	bananas, sliced
1 pound	apples, sliced
10 – 12	fresh mushrooms, sliced
2	oranges, peeled and sectioned
or	
2 (11-ounce) cans	mandarin oranges*
1 pint	strawberries, sliced (optional)
1	avocado, sliced (optional)
1 cup	Dressing

Combine spinach, bananas, apples, mushrooms and oranges. Add dressing to taste and toss lightly.

Dressing

1½ cups	sugar
2 teaspoons	dry mustard
2 teaspoons	salt
⅔ cup	white vinegar
3 tablespoons	onion juice
2 cups	vegetable oil
3 tablespoons	poppy seeds

In a blender, combine sugar, mustard, salt, and vinegar. Add onion juice and blend until smooth. Slowly add oil, blending until thick. Stir in poppy seeds. Store in the refrigerator if not used immediately. Serve with fresh fruit salads. Remaining dressing may be refrigerated for later use.

Mushroom and Mozzarella Salad with Basil Dressing

Serves 2

2 cups	mushrooms, sliced
2 small	tomatoes, sliced
1 cup	mozzarella cheese, cut into ¼-inch slices
	lettuce leaves

Dressing

1 small	clove garlic, crushed
⅓ cup	vegetable oil
2 tablespoons	lemon juice
2 tablespoons	white wine vinegar*
2 tablespoons	fresh basil, chopped
1 teaspoon	Worcestershire sauce
½ teaspoon	salt

Arrange mushrooms and tomatoes in shallow glass serving bowl and top with cheese. Mix dressing ingredients and pour over mushrooms, tomatoes and cheese. Cover and refrigerate one hour. Place lettuce on individual plates and top with marinated vegetables and cheese.

59

Black Bean Salad

2 (6.35-ounce) cans	black beans,* drained and rinsed
½ small	red bell pepper, finely chopped
½ small	yellow bell pepper, finely chopped
½ cup	green onions, sliced
½ cup	Chinese parsley,* chopped and firmly packed
2 teaspoons	virgin olive oil*
1 tablespoon	balsamic* or red wine vinegar*
1 tablespoon	fresh lemon juice
1 tablespoon	lemon rind, grated or slivered
½ teaspoon	chili powder
	salt and freshly ground pepper to taste
	Boston or Manoa* lettuce leaves

Combine black beans, red pepper, yellow pepper, green onions and Chinese parsley. Mix olive oil, vinegar, lemon juice, lemon rind and seasonings. Toss salad with dressing. Cover and chill, preferably overnight. Serve on a bed of lettuce.

Black beans may be found in the Oriental section of the supermarket and are not the same as Azuki beans

Fresh Tabouleh Salad

Serves 4

1 (5.25-ounce) package	tabouleh
1 bunch	fresh mint, chopped
1 bunch	fresh parsley, chopped
	salt and freshly ground pepper to taste
1 cup	cold water
4	plum tomatoes,* skinned, seeded and chopped
1	cucumber, chopped
½	red onion, chopped
1 cup	white beans, cooked and drained
4 tablespoons	olive oil*
4 tablespoons	lemon juice
	lettuce leaves

Combine tabouleh with mint, parsley, salt and pepper. Add water and let stand for 30 minutes. Stir in tomatoes, cucumber, onion, beans, olive oil and lemon juice. Cover and chill, preferably overnight. Serve on a bed of lettuce leaves.

Tarragon Potato Salad

Serves 4 – 6

The tarragon vinegar gives this potato salad a unique tangy flavor.

5 medium	white potatoes
¼ cup	vegetable oil
⅛ cup	tarragon vinegar*
⅓ cup	cold water
¾ teaspoon	salt
¼ teaspoon	freshly ground pepper
¾ cup	mayonnaise
¼ teaspoon	Tabasco
¼ teaspoon	dry mustard
¼ cup	onion, minced or grated
¼ cup	parsley, finely chopped

Peel and cut potatoes in half. Boil them until tender, approximately 25 minutes. Drain and cube them. Set aside. While potatoes are cooking, combine oil, vinegar, water, salt and pepper. Slowly stir the mayonnaise into the oil and vinegar mixture. Add the Tabasco, dry mustard, onion and parsley. Add warm cubed potatoes and toss gently. Cover and chill, preferably overnight.

Shrimp with Lime-Soy Vinaigrette

Serves 4

½ pound	medium to large shrimp, cooked, shelled and deveined
12	baby carrots, blanched
1½ cups	snow peas,* blanched
	Boston or Bibb lettuce leaves

Lime-Soy Vinaigrette

2 tablespoons	vegetable oil
½ teaspoon	lime zest
2 tablespoons	lime juice
1 tablespoon	soy sauce*
2 teaspoons	honey
dash	freshly ground pepper

Combine the dressing ingredients in a jar. Shake and chill overnight. Combine shrimp, carrots and pea pods. Cover and chill 2 hours or overnight. Arrange lettuce on individual serving plates and top with shrimp, carrots and pea pods. Drizzle vinaigrette over salad and serve.

Kakaako Coleslaw

1 (16-ounce) package	frozen peas, thawed
1 head	cabbage, thinly sliced
1/3 - 1/2 cup	almonds, slivered
2	green onions, chopped
1/2 small	carrot, sliced or shredded
1 stalk	celery, sliced or shredded (optional)
1 small	cucumber, sliced or shredded (optional)
1 (6-ounce) can	tuna, drained and flaked (optional)
1 (3-ounce) package	dried ramen noodles* with vegetable soup base, uncooked and broken into small pieces

Dressing

	vegetable soup base packet from noodles
1/3 cup	sugar
2/3 cup	vegetable oil
1 teaspoon	salt
dash	freshly ground pepper
6 tablespoons	rice vinegar*

Combine salad ingredients except for the noodles. Mix dressing ingredients and pour over salad. Toss salad with dressing. Cover and chill for at least 30 minutes. Top with noodle pieces and serve.

Mauna Kea* Fruit Salad

Serves 20

A mountain-sized salad packed with tropical fruit.

2	cantaloupes, cut into cubes or scooped into balls
1	honeydew melon, cut into cubes or scooped into balls
½ small	watermelon, cut into cubes or scooped into balls
1	pineapple,* cut into cubes
3	bananas, peeled and sliced crosswise
4	star fruits,* sliced crosswise
1 pound	seedless grapes
1 pint	strawberries, hulled
4	kumquats (optional)
3	kiwi fruits, peeled and sliced (optional)

Dressing

1 cup	sour cream
¼ cup	grated fresh coconut*
¼ cup	guava jelly*
2 tablespoons	dry white wine
½ cup	macadamia nuts,* chopped

Combine all fruits in a large bowl. In a small bowl, combine dressing ingredients. Serve dressing on the side.

The star fruit was introduced to Hawai'i by the Chinese. This translucent, yellow, star-shaped fruit possesses a delicate flavor, and its flesh is crisp and juicy. It is usually eaten fresh and cold, but also may be made into a juice. The star fruit is mainly available during the winter months.

65

Hearty Lentil Salad

Serves 10

1 pound	lentils
3	carrots, diced
½ pound	smoked turkey, diced
6 large	green onions, chopped
4 cups	mixed salad greens

Dressing

2 large cloves	garlic
1 cup	fresh parsley
⅓ cup	vegetable oil
¼ cup	fresh lemon juice
¼ cup	red wine vinegar*
2 tablespoons	Dijon mustard*
1 teaspoon	salt
1 teaspoon	grated lemon zest
½ teaspoon	freshly ground pepper

Bring a large saucepan of lightly salted water to a boil.
Add lentils and simmer until crisp-tender, about 20 – 30 minutes.
Add carrots and simmer for 2 more minutes. Meanwhile, mince
garlic in a food processor. Add parsley and finely chop. Add
remaining dressing ingredients and process until blended. Drain
lentils and combine with turkey and green onions. Pour dressing
over lentils and turkey and toss to coat. Arrange greens on
individual plates and divide lentil salad equally. Serve warm.

Three Bean Vinaigrette

Serves 10 – 12

1 (16-ounce) can	cut green beans, rinsed and drained
1 (15-ounce) can	red kidney beans, rinsed and drained
1 (15½-ounce) can	garbanzo beans, rinsed and drained
1 (6-ounce) can	pitted black olives, rinsed and drained
1	red onion, thinly sliced
1 medium	green bell pepper, minced

Dressing

½ cup	olive oil*
⅔ cup	red wine vinegar*
¼ cup	sugar
1 tablespoon	fresh basil, chopped
1 tablespoon	fresh parsley, chopped
3 cloves	garlic, pressed

Combine green beans, kidney beans, garbanzo beans, olives, onion and green pepper. Mix dressing ingredients and pour over salad, mixing lightly. Cover and chill, preferably overnight.

Island Chicken Salad

Serves 4

Serve this with a croissant for a great light lunch.

1½ cups	cooked white chicken or turkey meat, cut into chunks
¾ cup	celery, chopped
¼ cup	green onions, chopped
1 (6-ounce) can	water chestnuts,* drained and sliced
1 cup	seedless grapes
1 (8-ounce) can	pineapple chunks,* well drained
1 cup	mayonnaise
1 tablespoon	lemon juice
1¼ tablespoons	soy sauce*
1½ teaspoons	curry powder
1 tablespoon	mango chutney,* chopped
¼ cup	slivered almonds, toasted

Combine chicken, celery, green onions, water chestnuts, grapes and pineapple chunks. Mix mayonnaise, lemon juice, soy sauce, curry powder and chutney. Toss salad with dressing. Cover and chill, preferably overnight. Serve in papaya or pineapple halves, or on a bed of lettuce. Sprinkle with almonds before serving.

To toast almonds, place in a single layer on a baking sheet in a 350 degree oven for 10 minutes.

Summer Harvest Salad

Serves 8– 12

This may be made ahead and chilled for the perfect picnic salad.

1 – 1½ pounds	broccoli, raw or briefly steamed, cut into florets
1 medium	cauliflower, raw or briefly steamed, cut into florets
2 small	zucchini, sliced
2 pints	cherry tomatoes, trimmed
½ pound	fresh mushrooms, halved
2 bunches	green onions, chopped
1 cup	celery, diced
2 (5-ounce) cans	sliced water chestnuts,* drained
1 (6-ounce) can	pitted black olives, drained
2 cups	Swiss cheese, diced

Dressing

1 cup	mayonnaise
1 tablespoon	prepared horseradish
1 tablespoon	lemon juice
1 tablespoon	tarragon vinegar*
1½ teaspoons	dry mustard
1 clove	garlic, minced
	salt to taste
Garnish:	*Chopped parsley*

Combine salad ingredients. Mix dressing ingredients and pour over salad, mixing lightly. Garnish and serve.

Shrimp Salad

1 cup	crab meat
1 cup	medium to large shrimp, cooked, shelled and deveined
1 cup	fresh pineapple,* cut into 1-inch chunks
3 tablespoons	chutney*
1 cup	celery, sliced
¾ cup	scallions, including some of the tops, sliced
1 cup	water chestnuts,* sliced
½ cup	pine nuts or slivered almonds, toasted
¾ cup	mayonnaise
⅓ cup	sour cream
1 teaspoon	curry powder
	lettuce leaves

Combine crab meat, shrimp, pineapple, chutney, celery, scallions, water chestnuts and pine nuts or almonds and toss together lightly. Cover and refrigerate. In a small bowl, combine mayonnaise, sour cream, and curry, blending well. Cover and refrigerate for at least 2 hours. One hour before serving, pour mayonnaise mixture over salad and mix lightly but thoroughly. Return to refrigerator for 1 hour. Serve on a bed of lettuce.

Herbal Fruit Salad

Serves 6

This minty fruit salad tastes best the day that it is made.

6 cups	**assorted fresh fruit, cut into bite-size pieces**
1 tablespoon	**fresh mint, minced**
1 tablespoon	**fresh basil, minced**
2 tablespoons	**balsamic vinegar***

Combine fruit with mint, basil and vinegar. Cover and chill for 1 hour.

Hungarian Cucumber Salad

Serves 3

1 medium	**cucumber, sliced**
1 teaspoon	**salt**
3 tablespoons	**sour cream**
1 teaspoon	**vinegar**
1 teaspoon	**sugar**
¼ teaspoon	**dill weed**

Place cucumber slices on paper towels and lightly sprinkle with salt. Let stand for 10 minutes and lightly squeeze out the liquid. Combine sour cream, vinegar, sugar and dill. Toss cucumbers with dressing and serve.

Tomato-Ringed Brown Rice

Serves 6

3 cups	brown rice
2 cups	chicken broth
4 cups	water
½ cup	mayonnaise
3 (6-ounce) jars	marinated artichoke hearts, reserve marinade
½ cup	pimento-stuffed green olives, sliced
1 tablespoon	fresh basil, chopped
½	onion, finely chopped
3 stalks	celery, chopped
3	tomatoes, cut into wedges

In a saucepan, combine rice, chicken broth and water. Cover and let soak for 1 hour. Bring to a boil. Cover and simmer over low heat until liquid is absorbed, about 40 to 50 minutes. Combine mayonnaise with marinade from 2 jars of the artichoke hearts. Stir into the rice. Add artichoke hearts, olives, basil, onion and celery and toss to combine. Mound on a large serving platter and surround with tomato wedges. Serve at room temperature.

Greek Salad

1 head	red leaf lettuce, torn in bite-size pieces
2	tomatoes, cut into wedges
1	cucumber, peeled and sliced
1	green bell pepper, quartered, seeded and sliced
10	black olives
6 ounces	Feta cheese,* crumbled
6	radishes, sliced
6	green onions, sliced
2 tablespoons	parsley, chopped

Dressing

2 tablespoons	fresh lemon juice
8 tablespoons	olive oil*
¼ teaspoon	oregano
1 clove	garlic, crushed
	salt and freshly ground pepper to taste

Combine lettuce, tomatoes, cucumbers, green pepper, olives, cheese, radishes, green onions, and parsley. Combine the dressing ingredients in a jar. Shake until creamy and pour over salad. Toss well and serve immediately.

Hearts of Palm Salad

Serves 6

1 (16-ounce) can	hearts of palm, drained and cut in ½-inch pieces
6 cups	romaine lettuce, torn into bite-size pieces

Dressing

1 cup	olive oil*
½ cup	vinegar
½ cup	celery, finely chopped
¼ cup	red bell pepper, finely chopped
¼ cup	onion, finely chopped
¼ cup	dill pickles, finely chopped
6	black olives, finely chopped
2 cloves	garlic, pressed
¼ teaspoon	capers*

Combine dressing ingredients. Chill at least 8 hours. Arrange lettuce on individual serving plates and top with hearts of palm pieces. Pour dressing over salad and serve.

Confetti Salad

Serves 6

A crunchy, colorful salad.

2 (17-ounce) cans	whole kernel corn, drained
1 bunch	green onions, chopped
½ cup	celery, chopped
½ cup	green bell pepper, chopped
1 (2-ounce jar)	pimentos, drained and diced

Dressing

½ cup	vegetable oil
½ cup	vinegar
½ cup	sugar

Combine corn, green onions, celery, green pepper and pimentos. Bring dressing ingredients to a simmer in a medium saucepan. Pour over vegetables. Cover and refrigerate for at least 2 hours.

Chilled Tofu Salad

Serves 10

30 ounces	soft or medium tofu,* chilled and drained
3	green onions, finely diced
2 tablespoons	fresh ginger,* grated
10 teaspoons	light soy sauce*
	lettuce leaves

Drain tofu blocks and cut into ten equal slices. Place tofu on individual plates on a bed of lettuce. Top with equal portions of green onion, ginger and a teaspoon of soy sauce.

Fiesta Salad

2 bunches	broccoli, raw or briefly steamed, cut into florets
1 medium	cauliflower, raw or briefly steamed, cut into florets
2 cups	peas, briefly steamed
½ cup	red onion, chopped
½ large	red bell pepper, chopped
½ large	yellow bell pepper, chopped
1 cup	mozzarella cheese, cut into ¼-inch cubes

Dressing

1 teaspoon	Dijon mustard*
1 clove	garlic
1 cup	plain non-fat yogurt
⅓ cup	balsamic vinegar*
½ cup	olive oil* or canola oil*

In a blender, combine dressing ingredients and blend until smooth. Refrigerate for at least one hour before serving. Combine salad ingredients. Pour dressing over salad, toss and serve.

Curried Tuna Salad

Makes 3 cups

1 (6⅛-ounce) can	chunk light tuna, drained and flaked
½ cup	celery, diced
½ cup	carrot, diced
½ cup	raisins
½ cup	walnuts, chopped
¼ cup	green onion, chopped
½ cup	Swiss cheese, grated
1 teaspoon	fresh parsley, chopped
2 tablespoons	sweet pickle relish
½ cup	
plus	
2 tablespoons	mayonnaise
2 teaspoons	Dijon mustard*
¼ teaspoon	freshly ground pepper
½ teaspoon	salt
½ teaspoon	curry powder
½ cup	black olives, coarsely chopped
1	green bell pepper, chopped (optional)
1	red bell pepper, chopped (optional)
6	hard-cooked eggs,chopped (optional)
Garnish:	Parsley and alfalfa sprouts

Mix all ingredients. Cover and chill for 1 to 2 hours. Salad may be served with crackers or vegetables, stuffed into cucumbers or cherry tomatoes, or used as a sandwich spread.

Stuff tuna mixture into hollowed-out cucumber slices or cherry tomatoes using a melon baller or a small spoon.

Szechuan Noodle Salad with Eggplant

Serves 6

6	Japanese eggplants*
3 tablespoons	olive oil* or sesame oil*
1 (12-ounce) package	fresh Chinese noodles* or flat-noodle pasta, cooked and drained
1 cup	snow peas,* blanched
3 tablespoons	sesame seeds,* lightly toasted

Dressing

⅓ cup	sesame oil*
½ cup	tamari soy sauce*
3 tablespoons	balsamic vinegar*
2 tablespoons	sugar or maple syrup
2 tablespoons	chili oil*
8 to 10	green onions, thinly sliced
1 bunch	Chinese parsley,* chopped
1 tablespoon	fresh ginger,* finely chopped
3 cloves	garlic, minced
¼ teaspoon	red chili flakes (optional)
Garnish:	*Sesame seeds* and Chinese parsley*

Preheat the oven to 400 degrees. Pierce eggplants in several places and place on a baking sheet or glass pan. Drizzle oil over eggplant. Bake for 10 minutes. Turn eggplant over and bake an additional 10 minutes, until soft and the skins have shriveled. Slice the eggplant in half lengthwise. While the eggplant cools, prepare dressing. Combine dressing ingredients, stirring until the sugar is dissolved. In a large bowl, combine noodles with snow peas and sesame seeds. Add dressing and toss well to combine.

continued...

When eggplant is cool enough to handle, peel skin away from flesh and discard. Gently tear eggplant into strips. Add eggplant to salad mixture and mix thoroughly. Mound on a serving platter and garnish with additional sesame seeds and sprigs of Chinese parsley.

To toast sesame seeds, cook in a skillet over medium heat until they are lightly colored.

Maui Onion Salad Dressing

Makes ¾ cup

1 clove	garlic, pressed
¼	Maui onion,* sliced
½ cup	vegetable oil
¼ cup	sugar
¼ cup	vinegar
1	bay leaf, crumbled
1 teaspoon	salt
¼	prepared mustard
⅛ teaspoon	freshly ground pepper
⅛ teaspoon	Worcestershire sauce

In a food processor, mince garlic and Maui onion. Add remaining ingredients and blend until smooth. Chill for one hour before serving.

Sweet and Sour Zucchini Salad

Serves 6 – 8

½ cup	onion, minced
½ cup	wine vinegar*
½ cup	green bell pepper, chopped
½ cup	celery, chopped
6 small	zucchini, sliced paper-thin
¾ cup	sugar
1 teaspoon	salt
½ teaspoon	freshly ground pepper
⅓ cup	vegetable oil
⅔ cup	cider vinegar

Soak the onion in wine vinegar for ten minutes. Combine the green pepper, celery and zucchini. Add to the onion and vinegar. Mix sugar, salt, pepper, oil and cider vinegar. Pour over salad. Cover and chill overnight. Drain off marinade before serving.

Mandarin Spinach Salad

Serves 4 – 6

1 pound	**fresh spinach, washed, trimmed and torn in bite-size pieces**
6 slices	**bacon, fried crisp and crumbled**
1 cup	**slivered almonds, toasted**
1 small	**red onion, sliced into rings**
1 (11-ounce) can	**mandarin oranges***

Dressing

½ cup	**sugar**
2½ tablespoons	**vinegar**
2 tablespoons	**honey**
½ teaspoon	**lemon juice**
½ teaspoon	**onion salt**
½ teaspoon	**dry mustard**
½ teaspoon	**celery seed**
½ teaspoon	**paprika**
½ cup	**vegetable oil**

Combine spinach, bacon, almonds, onion and oranges. In a saucepan, mix sugar, vinegar, honey, lemon juice, onion salt, mustard, celery seed and paprika. Cook over low heat until sugar is dissolved. Stir in oil. Pour warm dressing over salad. Toss and serve immediately.

To toast almonds, place in a single layer on a baking sheet in a 350 degree oven for 10 minutes.

Watercress and Bacon Salad

Serves 6–8

2 cups	watercress* leaves, washed and torn into bite-size pieces
4 cups	fresh spinach, washed, trimmed and torn into bite-sized pieces
4 slices	bacon, fried and crumbled
1 cup	fresh mushrooms, thinly sliced

Dressing

1	egg
1½ tablespoons	lemon juice
1 tablespoon	white wine vinegar*
1 tablespoon	sugar
1 teaspoon	Dijon mustard*
	salt and freshly ground pepper to taste

Combine the watercress, spinach, bacon and mushrooms. Cover and refrigerate until ready to serve. In a saucepan, whisk egg, lemon juice, vinegar, sugar and mustard until thick and foamy. Cook over a medium-high heat, whisking constantly, until the dressing is thick and smooth. Do not allow to come to a boil. Immediately place saucepan in a pan filled with ice water. Whisk for one minute to cool slightly. Add salt and pepper to taste. Spoon slightly warm dressing over salad. Toss gently and serve immediately.

Fourth of July Potato Salad   *Serves 6*

Perfect for potlucks on those hot, humid summer days because there is no mayonnaise in this recipe.

2 pounds	**new potatoes, cooked and cut in ½-inch cubes**
½ cup	**green bell pepper, chopped**
¼ cup	**radishes or green onions, thinly sliced**
2 tablespoons	**fresh parsley, minced**
1 cup	**celery, chopped**

Dressing

¼ cup	**cider vinegar**
2 tablespoons	**vegetable oil**
2 tablespoons	**Dijon mustard***
½ teaspoon	**salt**
¼ teaspoon	**freshly ground pepper**
¼ teaspoon	**celery seed**

In a blender, combine dressing ingredients and blend until smooth. Refrigerate for at least one hour before serving. Combine potatoes, green pepper, radishes or green onions, parsley and celery. Pour dressing over salad and toss gently.

Ensalada de Noche Buena   *Serves 6*

4	oranges, peeled, sectioned and cut into bite-size pieces
¾ pound	jicama,* peeled and chopped
2	firm ripe bananas
2 tablespoons	Chinese parsley*
¼ cup	salted or unsalted peanuts, chopped
	seeds from 1 pomegranate
12	romaine lettuce leaves

Dressing

	juice and zest of 1 lime
¼ cup	reduced fat mayonnaise
2 tablespoons	honey
1 tablespoon	cider vinegar
¾ teaspoon	dried red chili pepper, ground or finely minced

In a blender, combine dressing ingredients and blend until smooth. Store in the refrigerator if not used immediately. Mix orange and jicama chunks together and refrigerate for 1 hour. Shortly before serving, peel and slice bananas. Add bananas and Chinese parsley to oranges and jicama chunks. Arrange lettuce leaves on individual plates or bowls and distribute salad evenly on top. Garnish with a sprinkling of peanuts and pomegranate seeds. Drizzle with dressing and serve.

Note: Very tart green apples, such as Granny Smith or Pippin, may be substituted for the jicama.

Russian Dressing

Makes 2 cups

4 cloves	garlic
1 cup	vegetable oil
½ cup	catsup
½ cup	sugar
½ cup	vinegar
1 inch slice	onion
4 teaspoons	parsley
1 teaspoon	oregano
1 teaspoon	basil
½ teaspoon	dry mustard
¼ teaspoon	celery seed
	salt and freshly ground pepper to taste

In a food processor, mince the garlic. Add remaining ingredients and blend until smooth. Refrigerate. Serve over a green salad.

Poppy Seed French Dressing

Makes 2 cups

1 cup	sugar
1 cup	vegetable oil
½ cup	white vinegar
1 teaspoon	dry mustard
1 teaspoon	celery seed
1 teaspoon	paprika
1 teaspoon	poppy seeds
1 teaspoon	salt
3 tablespoons	onion, grated

Combine all ingredients in blender. Blend until sugar is dissolved. Chill.

Sun Dried Tomato Dressing

Makes ½ cup

3 tablespoons	olive oil*
2 tablespoons	balsamic vinegar*
1 tablespoon	fresh basil, chopped
1 teaspoon	fresh dill, chopped
2 tablespoons	sun-dried tomatoes, packed in oil, diced and drained
½ teaspoon	salt

Combine ingredients in a jar and shake vigorously until blended. Refrigerate. Serve over a green salad.

Papaya Seed Dressing

Makes ¾ cup

Excellent on spinach salad.

½ cup	mayonnaise
2 tablespoons	vinegar
2 tablespoons	sugar
1 small	clove garlic
1 tablespoon	fresh papaya seeds*

Mix vinegar, mayonnaise and sugar in a blender. With motor running, add onion. Add papaya seeds and blend until the seeds resemble coarsely ground pepper. Chill for 1 hour before serving.

Sesame Dressing

Makes 2 cups

¼ cup	sesame oil*
¾ cup	oil
1 teaspoon	salt
2 cloves	garlic
¼ cup	onion, finely chopped
½ cup	lemon juice
3 tablespoons	honey
2 tablespoons	toasted sesame seeds,* divided

Blend all ingredients except for 1 tablespoon sesame seeds in a food processor or blender. Stir in remaining sesame seeds. Cover and refrigerate.

*It must be graduation time! And all those friends
and relatives will do their best to bury loved ones in
a fragrant and beautiful bounty of flower leis.*

Soups

Chilled Strawberry Soup   *Serves 4 – 6*

2 cups	fresh strawberries
½ cup	sour cream
2 cups	unsweetened pineapple* juice
⅓ cup	powdered sugar, sifted
½ cup	dry red wine
Garnish:	*Whipped cream, sliced strawberries, and mint*

Place strawberries in a food processor or blender and puree until smooth. Add sour cream and blend well. Add pineapple juice and sugar and process until mixture is creamy. Pour in wine and mix well. Cover and chill. Garnish.

Curried Avocado Soup   *Serves 6*

Creamy and rich.

1 (14½ ounce) can	chicken broth
⅔ cup	plain yogurt
2 cups	avocado
1 teaspoon	curry powder
2 cloves	garlic, crushed
¼ teaspoon	salt
¼ teaspoon	white pepper
Garnish:	*Sour cream and chopped chives*

Place all ingredients in a blender or food processor. Blend or process until smooth. Soup may be thinned with additional chicken broth or yogurt, if desired. Add curry powder, salt and white pepper to taste. Cover and chill. Garnish and serve.

Creamy Cucumber Soup
Makes 4 cups

Cool and refreshing.

2	**cucumbers, peeled and seeded**
1 clove	**garlic**
1 (14½-ounce) can	**chicken broth**
1 cup	**plain yogurt**
2 tablespoons	**white vinegar**
½ teaspoon	**salt**
Garnish:	*Chopped tomatoes, green onions and whole roasted almonds*

Place cucumbers, garlic and half of the chicken broth in a blender or food processor. Process until smooth. Add yogurt and blend well. Add remaining chicken broth, vinegar and salt. Blend. Cover and chill. Garnish and serve.

To remove seeds from the cucumbers, cut in half lengthwise and scoop out seeds.

Lahaina Gazpacho

4 – 5 large cloves	garlic, crushed
½ cup *plus*	
1 tablespoon	olive oil*
2 tablespoons	salt
6 tablespoons	wine or cider vinegar*
3 large slices	French bread, crumbled
1 teaspoon	white pepper
½ teaspoon	paprika
8 large	tomatoes, peeled and finely chopped
2 medium	green bell peppers, finely chopped
1 bunch	scallions (include tops), finely chopped
1 medium	red onion, finely chopped
2 large	cucumbers, peeled and finely chopped
2 cups	tomato juice
4 cups	water

Combine the garlic, oil, salt, vinegar, bread, white pepper, and paprika in a deep bowl. Add the chopped vegetables. In a separate bowl, combine the tomato juice and water and stir into the vegetable mixture. Cover and chill.

Sherried Pumpkin Soup

Serves 6

2 tablespoons	butter or margarine
½ cup	onion, finely chopped
1 teaspoon	fresh ginger,* minced
¼ teaspoon	nutmeg
2 (14½-ounce) cans	chicken broth
2¾ cups	canned pumpkin
½ cup	cream
3 tablespoons	dry sherry
¼ teaspoon	salt
⅛ teaspoon	freshly ground pepper
Garnish:	*Minced chives*

Sauté onions in butter until soft and translucent. Add ginger, nutmeg, and chicken broth and heat to boiling. Stir in pumpkin and cream. Reduce heat and simmer until heated through. Add sherry, salt and pepper. Garnish and serve.

Parmesan Spinach Soup   *Serves 6*

2 (10-ounce) packages	**frozen spinach**
or	
2 pounds	**fresh spinach, washed and trimmed**
4 tablespoons	**butter**
1 cup	**chicken broth**
2 cups	**milk**
¼ teaspoon	**nutmeg**
5 tablespoons	**fresh Parmesan cheese,* grated**
	salt
Garnish:	*Croutons*

Cook spinach in a covered saucepan for about 5 minutes. Drain, cool and coarsely chop. In a large saucepan sauté spinach in butter for 2 to 3 minutes. Add chicken broth, milk and nutmeg and bring to a boil. Reduce heat and simmer for 10 minutes, stirring frequently. Add Parmesan and simmer 1 to 2 minutes longer, stirring 2 or 3 times. Season with salt if desired. Garnish and serve.

Garden Herb-Zucchini Soup

Serves 4 – 6

6 medium	**zucchini, cut into 1-inch cubes**
	salt
2 tablespoons	**olive oil***
2 tablespoons	**unsalted butter**
1½ medium	**onions, chopped**
1 clove	**garlic, chopped**
5 cups	**chicken broth**
1 teaspoon	**oregano**
1 teaspoon	**fresh parsley, chopped**
2 teaspoons	**basil**
2 teaspoons	**fresh chives, chopped**
2 teaspoons	**lemon juice**
	freshly ground pepper to taste
Garnish:	*Sour cream*

Place zucchini cubes on paper towels and sprinkle with salt. Let stand for 10 minutes and lightly squeeze out the liquid. Meanwhile, sauté onion and garlic in oil and butter until soft and translucent, about 10 minutes. Do not brown the onions. Add zucchini and cook until tender, approximately seven minutes. Add chicken broth and simmer until zucchini are soft, about 15 minutes. Cool.

Note: This may be made ahead up to this point. Place mixture in a blender or food processor and process until smooth. Add herbs, lemon juice and pepper. Reheat and serve.

Pearl Barley Soup

Serves 8

¾ cup	pearl barley
3 cups	chicken broth
3 tablespoons	butter
1½ cups	onion, minced
1 cup	carrot, minced
1 cup	mushrooms, thinly sliced
½ cup	celery, minced
8 cups	chicken stock
	Salt and freshly ground pepper to taste
Garnish:	*Sour cream, sliced mushrooms and chopped parsley*

Bring barley and 3 cups chicken broth to a boil in a small saucepan. Reduce heat and simmer for 1 hour or until the liquid is absorbed. Sauté onion, carrot, mushrooms and celery in butter until tender. Add remaining chicken stock and simmer for 25 minutes. Add barley and simmer for five more minutes. Garnish and serve.

Shrimp Soup Orleans

Serves 4

1 (12-ounce) can	tomato juice
4 cups	chicken broth
⅓ cup	white wine
½ cup	yellow bell pepper, coarsely chopped
½ cup	diced tomatoes
⅓ cup	onion, chopped
½ cup	celery, chopped
1½ teaspoons	garlic, finely minced
8 drops	Tabasco
¼ teaspoon	coarsely ground black pepper
1 teaspoon	dried basil
¼ teaspoon	tarragon
⅛ teaspoon	paprika
1	bay leaf
1 pound	small shrimp, shelled and deveined
2 cups	cooked rice

In a large pot, bring the tomato juice, chicken broth, wine, yellow pepper, tomatoes, onion, celery, garlic, Tabasco and seasonings to a boil. Simmer over low heat for 15 minutes. Add shrimp and rice. Simmer until shrimp are pink and firm, about 10 minutes. Serve with French bread.

Oyster Artichoke Soup

Serves 8

4 tablespoons	butter
2 bunches	green onions, chopped
2 cloves	garlic, crushed
3 (6-ounce) jars	artichoke hearts, washed, drained and quartered
3 tablespoons	flour
4 (14½-ounce) cans	chicken broth
½ teaspoon	red pepper
1 teaspoon	anise
1 teaspoon	salt
1 tablespoon	Worcestershire sauce
1 quart	oysters

In a 4-quart pot, melt butter and sauté onions and garlic until soft and translucent. Add artichoke hearts. Sprinkle with flour and stir to coat well. Do not brown. Add broth, pepper and anise, salt and Worcestershire sauce. Simmer 15 minutes. Meanwhile, drain oysters and reserve liquid. Chop oysters in blender or food processor. Add oysters and reserved liquid to pot and simmer an additional 10 minutes. Do not boil. Soup may be made a day ahead and reheated prior to serving.

Variation: Clams may be used instead of oysters.

Coconut Mulligatawny Soup

Serves 6

This is an especially good use of leftover rice and chicken.

½ cup	onion, chopped
1	carrot, diced
2 stalks	celery, chopped
¼ cup	butter
1½ tablespoons	flour
2 teaspoons	curry powder
1	bay leaf
4 cups	chicken broth
¼ cup	Granny Smith or tart apples, finely chopped
½ cup	cooked rice
2 cups	cooked chicken, diced
	salt and freshly ground pepper to taste
½ cup	coconut milk,* heated

Sauté onions, carrot, and celery in butter until soft and tender but do not brown. Stir in flour and curry powder. Cook about 3 minutes. Add bay leaf and chicken broth and simmer 15 minutes. Add apples, rice and chicken and simmer another 15 minutes. Add salt and pepper to taste. Stir in hot coconut milk immediately before serving.

Variation: Hot cream may be used instead of coconut milk.

Sausage Minestrone

Serves 6 – 8

Great for Monday night football.

½ pound	Italian sausage, casing removed
1 cup	onion, coarsely chopped
½ cup	carrots, peeled and coarsely chopped
½ cup	celery, coarsely chopped
4 tablespoons	parsley, chopped
2 (14½-ounce) cans	Italian-style tomatoes, broken with a fork
2 (14½-ounce) cans	chicken broth
1 teaspoon	basil
½ cup	spaghetti, broken into pieces
	salt and freshly ground pepper to taste
Garnish:	Freshly grated Parmesan cheese*

In a saucepan, brown the sausage, breaking it up into bite-size pieces as it cooks. Remove sausage, using drippings to sauté the onion until tender. Discard drippings. Add the sausage, vegetables, chicken broth and basil to the saucepan and bring to a boil. Cook over medium heat for 15 minutes. Add spaghetti pieces, salt and pepper. Reduce heat, cover and simmer for 20 minutes. Garnish and serve.

Vangie's Clam Stew

Serves 8 – 10

The bacon and drippings enhance this soup's flavor.

3	potatoes, diced
1 (8-ounce) package	frozen mixed vegetables, thawed
1½	celery stalks, diced
1 medium	onion, chopped
1	tablespoon dried parsley
1 teaspoon	dill weed
	salt and freshly ground pepper to taste
1 teaspoon	Old Bay seasoning*
1 (8-ounce) can	tomato sauce
1 (6.5-ounce) can	minced clams
½ pound	bacon, diced
1 handful	noodles or pasta

Combine all ingredients except the bacon and noodles and cook until vegetables are tender, about 20 to 30 minutes. Fry bacon and add both bacon and drippings to the soup. Add noodles and cook until tender, about 5 minutes.

Mediterranean Fish Stew   *Serves 6*

2 tablespoons	olive oil*
1 large	onion, chopped
1 large	carrot, peeled and chopped
3 cloves	garlic, minced
1 (6-ounce) can	tomato paste
¾ cup	dry white wine
1 cup	water
	salt and freshly ground pepper to taste
2 teaspoons	dried basil
½ teaspoon	dried red chili pepper
2 pounds	firm white fish fillets (turbot, snapper, haddock, halibut, sole, orange roughy, etc.)
Garnish:	*Chopped parsley*

In a large Dutch oven or flame-proof casserole dish, sauté onion and carrot in oil until tender. Add garlic, tomato paste, wine, water and seasonings. Cover and simmer for 30 minutes. Preheat oven to 375 degrees. Arrange fish fillets on top of tomato-vegetable sauce and bake for 20 to 30 minutes. Garnish with parsley.

Italian Clam Stew

⅓ cup	olive oil*
1	onion, chopped
4 cloves	garlic, minced
1 teaspoon	dried basil
or	
6 leaves	fresh basil, minced
1 teaspoon	dried oregano
1 (6-ounce) can	tomato paste
¼ cup	white wine
1½ cups	water
	salt and freshly ground pepper to taste
40	littleneck clams, rinsed

Sauté onion and garlic in olive oil until soft and translucent. Add remaining ingredients except for clams and bring to a boil. Season, reduce heat and simmer for 5 minutes. Add clams, cover and simmer, stirring occasionally, until clams open, about 5 to 10 minutes.

Flying paper koi or Japanese carp flutter above many island homes to honor Boys' Day on the fifth day of the fifth month. The carp fights its way upstream showing the determination, strength and courage a family hopes each boy of theirs will share.

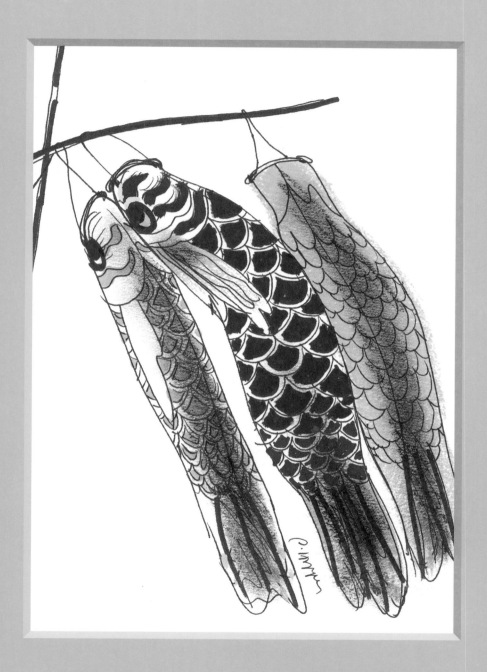

Breads

Quick

Yeast

Bran-ana Muffins

Makes one dozen

These healthy muffins freeze well.

¾ cup	flour
¾ cup	whole wheat flour
½ cup	unprocessed oat bran, uncooked
2 teaspoons	baking powder
½ teaspoon	baking soda
¼ teaspoon	salt
1 teaspoon	cinnamon
1	egg
¾ cup	brown sugar
1⅓ cups	mashed ripe bananas, mashed
½ cup	raisins
or	
½ cup	walnuts, chopped
⅓ cup	vegetable oil
1 teaspoon	vanilla extract

Preheat oven to 375 degrees. Grease muffin pans or line with paper baking cup liners. In a large bowl, combine flours, bran, baking powder, baking soda, salt, and cinnamon. Make a well in the center of the dry ingredients and set aside. Combine egg and brown sugar and beat until smooth. Add bananas, raisins, oil and vanilla and beat well. Pour into well in flour mixture all at once, stirring just until dry ingredients are moistened. Fill muffin cups ⅔ full with batter. Bake for 20 to 25 minutes. Remove from pans immediately.

Granny's
Apple Coffee Cake

Serves 10

2 cups	apples, peeled, seeded and coarsely diced
1	egg, beaten
¼ cup	vegetable oil
1 cup	sugar
2 teaspoons	cinnamon
¼ teaspoon	nutmeg
½ cup	walnuts, chopped
1 cup	flour
½ teaspoon	salt
1 teaspoon	baking soda

Preheat oven to 350 degrees. Grease and flour an 8 x 8-inch pan. Combine apples, egg, and oil. Add sugar, cinnamon, nutmeg and walnuts. Stir until blended. Sift dry ingredients and stir into apple mixture. Pour into pan and bake for 40 minutes.

Note: Use Granny Smith or Rome apples for best results.

Feather-Weight Coffee Cake

A light and easy coffee cake.

4 teaspoons	butter or margarine, melted
1	egg, beaten
½ cup	milk
1 cup	flour
¾ cup	sugar, divided
3 teaspoons	baking powder
½ teaspoon	salt
¼ cup	sugar
1 teaspoon	cinnamon

Preheat oven to 375 degrees. Grease an 8-inch square pan. Mix butter, egg and milk in a small bowl. Combine flour, ½ cup sugar, baking powder and salt and sift 3 times. Add dry ingredients to milk mixture and mix together just enough to combine smoothly. Pour into prepared pan. Combine ¼ cup sugar and cinnamon and sprinkle over cake. Bake for 12 to 15 minutes. Serve immediately as is or with butter and jelly.

Cereal Nut Bread

Makes one loaf

1½ cups	flour
2½ teaspoons	baking powder
¼ teaspoon	salt
1 cup	ripe bananas, mashed
⅔ cup	brown sugar
⅓ cup	orange juice
1	egg, slightly beaten
⅓ cup	butter, melted and slightly cooled
2 cups	fortified oat flake cereal
¾ cup	pecans or walnuts, coarsely chopped

Preheat oven to 350 degrees. Grease a 9 x 5 x 3-inch loaf pan. Sift dry ingredients together. Add bananas, brown sugar, orange juice, egg and butter. Mix only enough to moisten flour. Stir in cereal and pecans and pour batter into pan. Bake for 50 minutes. Cool in pan for 10 minutes, then turn out on a wire rack for further cooling.

Family Pumpkin Bread

Makes two large or three medium loaves

2⅔ cup	sugar
⅔ cup	shortening
4	eggs
1 pound	canned pumpkin
⅔ cup	water
3⅓ cups	flour
2 teaspoons	baking soda
1½ teaspoons	salt
½ teaspoon	baking powder
1 teaspoon	cinnamon
1 teaspoon	cloves
⅔ cup	walnuts
⅔ cup	golden raisins
3 tablespoons	powdered sugar

Preheat oven to 350 degrees. Grease and flour two 9 x 5 x 3-inch (or three 8½ x 4½-inch) loaf pans. Cream sugar and shortening until fluffy. Stir in eggs, pumpkin and water. Combine dry ingredients and stir into pumpkin mixture. Add walnuts and golden raisins and pour into pans. Bake for 1 hour and 10 minutes or until toothpick inserted in center of loaf comes out clean. Cool on wire rack. Sprinkle top with powdered sugar.

Note: For a cookie bar, bake in a 9 x 13-inch pan.

Blue Ribbon
Banana Bread

Makes 2 loaves

3	eggs
½ cup	vegetable oil
½ cup	butter or margarine, melted
1½ cups	sugar
2 cups	flour (may use 1 cup whole wheat and 1 cup all-purpose)
2 teaspoons	baking soda
½ teaspoon	salt
pinch	cinnamon
2 cups	bananas, sliced and firmly packed
1 teaspoon	vanilla
2 cups	walnuts, chopped

Preheat oven to 350 degrees. Grease and flour two
8½ x 4½ x 2½-inch loaf pans. Beat eggs, oil, butter and sugar
for 2 minutes. Add dry ingredients and mix well. Add bananas
and vanilla and mix until bananas are mashed. Add nuts. Pour
into prepared pans and bake for 50 to 55 minutes or until a
toothpick comes out clean. Remove from pans immediately and
cool on a wire rack.

Note: For terrific mango bread, substitute 2 cups drained
mangos for the bananas and add 2 teaspoons cinnamon.

*The first Hawaiians brought the Hawaiian banana plant to the islands
from the South Pacific. It now grows wild in mountain valleys. Today
the most common and most delectable varieties grown in Hawai'i are the
Chinese, Bluefield, and the Brazilian Apple bananas. They grow in
warm, moist areas and ripen year round, one bunch to a tree. Bananas
are usually eaten raw but also may be cooked ripe or green, as substitute
for white or sweet potatoes.*

Japanese Rice Crackers *(Arare)*

Makes 6 – 8 cups

An island snack time favorite.

1½ cups	flour
1½ cups	mochiko* flour
3 tablespoons	sugar
2 tablespoons	black sesame seeds*
2 tablespoons	baking powder
1 cup	water
	vegetable oil for deep frying

Combine flour, mochiko flour, sugar, sesame seeds, baking powder and water. Add more water if necessary to make dough stick together. Divide dough into 4 parts and roll each paper thin on floured board. Cut in 1-inch squares. Heat the oil to 375 degrees in a deep-fat fryer or heavy kettle. Fry crackers in batches, turning once, until golden brown, about 2 to 3 minutes per batch. Drain on paper towels.

Glaze

¼ cup	corn syrup
¼ cup	sugar
¼ cup	soy sauce*

Preheat oven to 300 degrees. Combine corn syrup, sugar and soy sauce and bring to a boil. Cook glaze until it falls thick from spoon. Pour on cooled rice crackers and mix. Place crackers in a single layer on cookie sheets and bake for 15 to 20 minutes or until dry.

Portuguese Malasadas

Makes 3 dozen

Malasadas are traditionally eaten on Shrove Tuesday, before the start of Lent.

2½ teaspoons	active dry yeast
1 teaspoon	sugar
⅓ cup	warm water
6 cups	flour
1 cup	sugar
1 teaspoon	salt
1 cup	milk
1	potato, cooked and mashed
⅔ cup	water
⅓ cup	butter, melted
5	eggs, beaten
	vegetable oil for deep frying
	sugar

Mix yeast with 1 teaspoon sugar and add to warm water. Let stand for 5 minutes. Mix flour, sugar and salt in a large bowl. Stir in milk, potato and water. Add butter, eggs and yeast mixture and mix well. Cover and let dough rise for 2 hours in a warm spot. Heat 2 to 3 inches of oil in a deep fryer to 375 degrees. Dip fingertips in bowl of oil or softened butter, then pinch off golf ball-size pieces of raised dough. Drop in heated oil and cook until golden brown on one side. Turn over and fry until golden brown on the other side. Drain on paper towels and roll in sugar. Serve immediately.

Cinnamon Swirl
Raisin Bread

Makes 2 loaves

8 cups	**flour**
1 package	
(1 tablespoon)	**active dry yeast**
2 cups	**milk**
¼ cup	**sugar**
¼ cup	**butter**
2 teaspoons	**salt**
3	**eggs**
½ cup	**sugar**
2 teaspoons	**ground cinnamon**
2 cups	**raisins, soaked until softened**

Combine 3 cups flour and yeast in a large bowl. In a saucepan, heat milk, sugar, butter, and salt until warm (115 – 120 degrees) and butter is almost melted, stirring constantly. Add to flour mixture and add eggs. Beat at low speed of electric mixer ½ minute, scraping bowl. Beat at high speed until smooth, about 3 minutes. Mix in enough of the remaining flour to make dough stiff enough to pull away from the sides of the bowl with a wooden spoon. Stir in raisins. Turn out onto a lightly floured surface. Knead until dough is smooth and elastic, about 6 to 8 minutes. Add remaining flour as necessary. Shape into a ball. Place in a lightly greased bowl and turn once to grease top. Cover loosely with clear plastic wrap or a damp cloth. Let rise in a warm place until doubled (about 1¼ hours). Punch down dough. Divide dough in half. Cover and let rest for 10 minutes. Roll each half of the dough on a lightly floured surface into 15 x 7-inch rectangle. Brush dough lightly with water. Combine sugar and cinnamon and sprinkle over dough. Beginning with the narrow end, roll up tightly. Pinch edge of dough into roll to seal well. Press each end with side of hand to seal and fold

continued...

ends under. Place loaves seam sides down in 2 greased 9 x 5 x
3-inch loaf pans. Cover and let rise until nearly double, about
35 to 45 minutes. Preheat oven to 375 degrees. Bake for 35 to
45 minutes, covering with foil during last 15 minutes to prevent
over-browning. Remove from pans and cool on a wire rack.
Drizzle with icing.

Icing

1 cup	powdered sugar, sifted
¼ teaspoon	vanilla
1 teaspoon	milk

Combine powdered sugar, vanilla and milk. Blend until smooth.

Sweet Cornbread

The sugar adds a hint of sweetness to this bread.

½ cup	butter
1 cup	sugar
2	eggs
2 cups	flour
6 tablespoons	cornmeal
3 teaspoons	baking powder
½ teaspoon	salt
¼ teaspoon	baking soda
1 cup	milk

Preheat oven to 350 degrees. Grease a 9 x 13-inch baking
pan. Cream butter and sugar until fluffy. Blend in eggs.
Combine dry ingredients and stir into creamed mixture. Add milk
and mix well. Pour into prepared pan. Bake for 30 to 35
minutes. While cornbread is still warm, spread top generously
with soft butter.

Kahuku Ranch Bread

Makes 2 loaves

This bread is excellent for toasting.

5½ – 6 cups	flour
2 packages (2 tablespoons)	active dry yeast
1 tablespoon	sugar
2 teaspoons	salt
¼ teaspoon	baking soda
2 cups	milk
½ cup	water
	corn meal

Combine 3 cups flour, yeast, sugar, salt and baking soda. Heat milk and water until very warm (120 to 130 degrees) and add to dry ingredients. Beat well. Stir in enough flour to make a stiff batter. Dough is ready to knead when it is stiff enough to pull away from sides of the bowl with a wooden spoon. Turn onto floured board and knead until smooth and elastic. Add more flour if dough is sticky. Divide dough in half and shape into loaves. Place loaves into two 9 x 5 x 3-inch loaf pans which have been oiled and sprinkled with corn meal. Cover and let rise in a warm place until double, about 45 minutes. Preheat oven to 400 degrees. Bake for 25 minutes. Turn loaves out onto rack to cool.

Cooked
Cornmeal Rolls

Makes 18 – 30 rolls

1 package (1 tablespoon)	**active dry yeast**
¼ cup	**lukewarm water**
⅓ cup	**cornmeal**
½ cup	**sugar**
1 teaspoon	**salt**
½ cup	**shortening**
2 cups	**milk**
2	**egg whites, beaten**
5 cups	**flour**

Soften yeast in water. Cook cornmeal, sugar, salt, shortening, and milk in a double boiler until thick, stirring often. Cool to lukewarm and add egg whites and yeast. Beat thoroughly and let rise one hour. Add 4 cups flour, one cup at a time. Turn out onto a floured board and knead in the fifth cup of flour. Shape into a ball. Place in a lightly greased bowl and turn once to grease top. Cover loosely with clear plastic wrap or a damp cloth. Let rise in a warm place until doubled. Punch down dough. Grease and flour two 9 or 10-inch pie pans or two 1½ to 2-quart round casseroles. Divide the dough in half. Each half of the dough will fill 1 pan or casserole. Cut each half of the dough into 10 to 15 pieces. Shape each piece into a ball and place into prepared pans. Let rise for 1 hour. Preheat oven to 375 degrees. Bake until browned, about 25 minutes. A toothpick inserted into a middle roll will come out dry. Remove from pans and cool on racks for about 20 minutes before serving.

Honey Oatmeal Bread   *Makes 2–3 loaves*

This bread is light and chewy with a subtly sweet flavor.

1¾ cups	water
½ cup	cracked wheat or bulgur (may use steel cut oats)
2 packages (2 tablespoons)	active dry yeast
½ cup	warm water
1 cup	rolled oats
⅓ cup	margarine
½ cup	honey
1 teaspoon	salt
2	eggs, beaten
5 – 6 cups	flour

Place 1¾ cups water in saucepan and bring to a boil. Remove from heat and add cracked wheat. Let soften for 5 minutes. Combine yeast and ½ cup warm water, stirring until dissolved. Place oats, margarine, honey and salt in a large mixing bowl. Add the water and softened wheat and stir until well blended and margarine and honey have melted. Add eggs and mix thoroughly. Stir in yeast mixture. Add the flour one cup at a time to make a stiff dough. Turn dough out onto floured board. Sprinkle dough with flour and knead until smooth and no longer sticky, approximately 5 minutes. Cover and let rise in a warm place until doubled, approximately 45 minutes to 1 hour. Punch down dough, knead briefly and shape into 2 large or 3 medium sized loaves. Place in greased 9 x 5 x 3-inch loaf pans or on a cookie sheet. Cover and let rise in a warm place until double in size. Preheat oven to 350 degrees. Bake for 40 to 45 minutes for medium sized loaves or 45 to 55 minutes for large sized loaves, or until golden brown. Remove from pans and cool on wire racks before slicing.

Gingerbread

A quick, easy after-school treat.

½ cup	**butter**
½ cup	**sugar**
1	**egg, beaten**
1 cup	**molasses**
2½ cups	**flour**
1½ teaspoons	**baking soda**
1 teaspoon	**cinnamon**
1½ teaspoons	**ground ginger**
1 teaspoon	**ground cloves**
½ teaspoon	**salt**
1 cup	**hot water**
Garnish:	*Whipped cream*

Preheat oven to 350 degrees. Cream butter and sugar. Add molasses and egg. Set aside. Sift together dry ingredients and add to butter mixture. Blend well. Add hot water and beat until smooth. Bake in a 9-inch square pan for 35 to 40 minutes.

O-bon, Festival of Joy.
A Buddhist Celebration of
true giving and remembrance.
Dance, eat saimin and barbecued meat.

Poultry

Seafood

Entrées

Bombay Chicken

Serves 4– 6

A delightful change for chicken.

6	chicken breasts, skinned
1 cup	chunky peanut butter
1 cup	Dijon mustard*
2 tablespoons	tarragon
1½ cups	orange marmalade
¼ cup	olive oil*
1 tablespoon	curry powder
1	lime, sliced

Combine peanut butter, mustard, tarragon, marmalade, olive oil, curry powder and lime. Add chicken, cover and marinate overnight in the refrigerator. Broil 6 inches from heat for 10 to 15 minutes on each side or until the juices run clear when the breast is pierced with a fork.

Chicken Lychee

Serves 6

1½ teaspoons	salt
2 teaspoons	sugar
2 tablespoons	fresh ginger,* minced
4 teaspoons	soy sauce*
2 tablespoons	sherry
2 pounds	boneless chicken breasts, skinned and cut in bite-size pieces
2 tablespoons	peanut oil*
4 teaspoons	cornstarch
2 tablespoons	water
¼ cup	green onions, minced
1 tablespoon	Chinese parsley,* minced
1 (20-ounce) can	lychee,*
or	
1½ cups	fresh lychee,* pitted and peeled
1 (11-ounce) can	mandarin oranges*
⅔ cup	almonds, slivered and toasted

Combine salt, sugar, ginger, soy sauce and sherry. Add chicken and marinate one hour or overnight. Heat peanut oil in a large skillet and brown chicken. Dissolve cornstarch in water and add to skillet. Add onions and parsley. Cover and simmer for 10 minutes. Remove from heat and stir in oranges, almonds and lychee. Serve immediately over rice.

The first lychee tree was brought to Hawai'i in 1873 and was planted in Nu'uanu, where it still stands today. Originally from South China, the tree provides thick foliage for shade as well as small bunches of red fruit. The rough outer skin covers a juicy grape-like pulp and one black seed. Lychee season runs from June to July, and one tree may produce up to 200 pounds of fruit.

Sausalito Chicken

An easy dish using fresh spring mushrooms.

4 large	boneless chicken breasts
¾ teaspoon	seasoned salt
1 (6-ounce) jar	marinated artichoke hearts
1 tablespoon	flour
½ cup	water
¼ cup	dry white wine or vermouth
1	chicken bouillon cube, crumbled
12 small	fresh mushrooms, halved

Salt chicken. Drain artichoke hearts, reserving the marinade. Cut artichoke hearts in half. Brown chicken in 3 tablespoons of the artichoke marinade. Remove chicken and add remaining marinade, flour, water, wine and bouillon. Stir gently until mixture boils and thickens slightly. Stir in artichokes and mushrooms and chicken. Cover and simmer for 20 minutes. Serve over rice.

Cornish Hens with Wild Rice

4 tablespoons	butter, divided
2 cups	fresh mushrooms, thinly sliced
1 cup	celery, finely diced
⅔ cup	green onion, including tops, finely chopped
1 cup	wild rice, cooked
½ cup	sour cream
4 (1-pound)	Cornish game hens
½ teaspoon	salt

Preheat oven to 350 degrees. In a medium skillet, melt 2 tablespoons butter over low heat. Sauté mushrooms, celery and onions until tender but not brown. Add cooked rice and sour cream and mix well. Stuff hens with rice mixture, using about ½ cup in each. Place any unused rice stuffing in a baking dish. Close openings with skewers. Place hens breast sides up on rack in a shallow baking pan. Melt 2 tablespoons butter and brush over hens. Sprinkle with salt. Bake hens until golden brown and tender, about 1 hour, basting occasionally. Bake rice stuffing, covered, for last 30 minutes of baking time.

Country Supper

Serves 6

A complete meal in a steaming foil package.

3 medium	potatoes, cut into ½-inch slices
6	chicken thighs or breasts, skinned (about 2 pounds)
	salt and freshly ground pepper to taste
3	carrots; cut into chunks
6 small	cloves garlic, crushed
1 pound	green beans, cut up
3 medium	onions, quartered
6 tablespoons	dry white wine or water
½ teaspoon	thyme
6	fresh rosemary sprigs
2	bay leaves, crumbled

Preheat oven to 350 degrees. Cut 6 pieces of foil 16 inches long. In the center of each piece, place ⅙ of the potatoes and 1 piece of chicken. Season with salt and pepper. Evenly divide the carrots, green beans, garlic and onions and add to the foil. Sprinkle with wine, thyme, rosemary and bay leaves. Bring the edges of the foil together and fold over. Tightly fold ends over and seal. Place on a baking sheet and bake for 50 minutes or until chicken and vegetables are tender.

Glazed Curry Turkey

½ cup	honey
½ cup	mustard
¼ cup	butter, melted
½ teaspoon	salt
1 teaspoon	curry powder
1½ pounds	boneless turkey breast
	sesame seeds*
Garnish:	*Parsley*

Preheat oven to 350 degrees. Place the turkey on a rack in a shallow baking pan. Mix honey, mustard, butter, salt and curry powder. Pour ¼ of marinade over turkey. Bake at 350 degrees for 15 minutes and then drain off fat. Pour rest of marinade over turkey and bake about 15 minutes more. Baste again and sprinkle with sesame seeds. Broil for about 2 minutes. Garnish with parsley.

Poulet Dijon

3 pounds	**boneless chicken breasts, skinned**
3 tablespoons	**butter**
2 tablespoons	**flour**
1 cup	**chicken broth**
½ cup	**half and half**
2 tablespoons	**Dijon mustard***
¼ teaspoon	**salt**
¼ teaspoon	**white pepper**
Garnish:	*Tomato wedges and parsley*

Sauté chicken in butter over medium heat for 12 to 15 minutes. Transfer chicken to a plate and keep warm. Stir flour into pan drippings. Slowly add broth and cream, stirring until mixture bubbles and thickens. Stir in mustard, salt and pepper. Pour sauce over chicken and garnish with tomato wedges and parsley.

Chicken Assaggio

Serves 2

6 tablespoons	extra virgin olive oil*
½ pound	boneless chicken, skinned and cut into bite-sized pieces
	salt and freshly ground pepper to taste
2 cloves	garlic, chopped
½ teaspoon	basil
6 medium	pepperoncini,* cut into strips
½ cup	green bell pepper, roasted and cut into strips
½ cup	mushrooms, sliced
¼ cup	black olives, sliced
1 teaspoon	capers*
¼ cup	dry white wine
¼ cup	butter
8 ounces	linguine or spaghettini, cooked
Garnish:	*Fresh chopped parsley and fresh chopped basil*

Heat olive oil in a large skillet. Add chicken and stir-fry for 3 to 5 minutes. Add salt, pepper, garlic and basil. Cook for another 2 minutes. Add pepperoncini, sweet roasted pepper, mushrooms, black olives and capers. Cook, stirring until the vegetables are barely tender. Reduce heat to low and stir in wine and butter. Serve over pasta. Garnish with fresh parsley and basil.

To roast bell pepper, halve lengthwise and remove the seeds. Place pieces lengthwise on a broiler pan. Broil peppers until brown blisters appear on the skin. Peel and slice into strips.

Rosemary Chicken

Serves 4

A hearty dish for company.

3 – 4 pounds	**whole chicken fryer, cut up**
1 tablespoon	**butter**
1 tablespoon	**vegetable oil**
	salt and freshly ground pepper
	to taste
2 – 3 cloves	**garlic, crushed**
½ cup	**white wine**
½ tablespoons	**dried rosemary**
or	
1 tablespoon	**fresh rosemary**
3 slices	**bacon, fried and cut into 2-inch**
	pieces
2 tablespoons	**tomato paste**
½ cup	**chicken broth**

Brown chicken pieces in butter and oil. Add salt, pepper and garlic when the chicken is almost browned. When the chicken is completely browned, add wine, rosemary and bacon. Cover and cook for 15 minutes. Combine tomato paste and chicken broth and add to the pan. Cover and cook until chicken is tender, about 30 minutes.

Drunken Chicken Kabobs   *Serves 8*

¼ cup	bourbon
¼ cup	soy sauce*
¼ cup	Dijon mustard*
¼ cup	brown sugar
½ cup	onion, chopped
½ teaspoon	pepper
dash	Worcestershire sauce
1½ pounds	chicken thighs, boned and cut into 1-inch cubes
1	green bell pepper, cut into 1-inch pieces
1	red bell pepper, cut into 1-inch pieces
2	onions, cut into 1-inch pieces
8	cherry tomatoes
8 small	mushrooms
16	pineapple* chunks

In a shallow dish, combine the bourbon, soy sauce, mustard, brown sugar, onion, pepper and Worcestershire sauce. Add chicken and vegetables and marinate, covered, for at least 2 hours. Drain, reserving the marinade. Place peppers and onions in a microwave-safe dish and cook on high for 1 minute. Thread the chicken, peppers, onions, cherry tomatoes, mushrooms and pineapple alternately onto skewers. Place skewers on a rack in a large broiler pan. Brush with marinade and broil until chicken is cooked, about 12 minutes. Turn the kabobs 2 or 3 times during the cooking process and brush frequently with marinade.

Tijuana Torte

Try this instead of nachos.

1 pound	**ground turkey**
1	**medium onion, chopped**
1 (16-ounce) can	**stewed tomatoes, coarsely chopped**
1 (8-ounce) can	**tomato sauce**
1 (4-ounce) can	**chopped green chilies**
1 (1.25-ounce) package	**taco seasoning mix**
12	**corn tortillas**
1 pound	**cheddar cheese, grated**
Garnish:	*Sour cream*

Preheat oven to 350 degrees. Brown ground turkey and onion in skillet. Add stewed tomatoes, tomato sauce, chilies and taco seasoning mix. Combine thoroughly and simmer 10 to 15 minutes. Place about ¼ cup of tomato-meat mixture in bottom of 9 x 13-inch baking dish. Place 2 tortillas side by side on top of the tomato and meat mixture. Top each with some meat and tomatoes and grated cheese. Repeat until each stack contains six tortillas layered with meat and tomatoes and cheese. Bake at 350 degrees for 20 to 25 minutes or until cheese is bubbly.

Sesame Chicken

6	**chicken thighs, boned and cut into 1 – 1½-inch cubes**
	cornstarch
	peanut oil

Sauce

¼ cup	**soy sauce***
¼ cup	**sugar**
1 tablespoon	**sesame seeds,* toasted**
1-inch piece	**fresh ginger,* finely grated**
2	**green onions, finely sliced**
½ – 1 teaspoon	**sesame oil***
Garnish:	*Chopped green onions*

Coat chicken thoroughly with cornstarch and refrigerate for at least 1 hour. Coat again lightly just before frying. In a saucepan, mix soy sauce, sugar, sesame seeds and ginger. Cook over low heat until sugar is dissolved. Stir in green onions and sesame oil. Deep fry the chicken pieces in peanut oil at 350 degrees for 3 minutes or until light golden brown. Drain and dip in sauce. Serve over rice. Spoon on any unused sauce and garnish with green onions

To toast sesame seeds, cook them in a skillet over medium heat until they are lightly colored.

Hawaiian Chicken Curry   *Serves 4*

1 small	onion, finely chopped
1 clove	garlic, minced
1 teaspoon	fresh ginger,* minced
7 tablespoons	butter, divided
1 tablespoon	curry powder
1 teaspoon	sugar
½ teaspoon	salt
3 cups	coconut milk*
¼ cup	flour
1½ pounds	boneless chicken, cut into bite-size pieces

Sauté onion, garlic and ginger in 2 tablespoons of butter until onion is translucent. Stir in curry powder, sugar, and salt and blend well. Slowly pour in coconut milk, stirring constantly. Reduce heat and simmer for 20 minutes. Strain. Melt 4 tablespoons of butter in a skillet. Stir in flour to make a smooth paste. Add curry sauce and bring to a low boil, stirring constantly. Cook until thickened. Heat remaining tablespoon butter in another skillet and sauté chicken until brown. Add curry sauce and cook until heated through. Serve with fluffy white rice and assorted condiments from the following list.

Curry Condiments:

Chopped bananas	Diced avocado
Chutney	Chopped green bell pepper
Grated hard-cooked eggs	Diced tomatoes
Chopped green onions	Black olives
Shredded coconut	Plain yogurt
Raisins	Chopped macadamia nuts
Chopped bacon	Chopped cucumbers

Chicken Soft Tacos

Serves 5–6

1½ cups	sour cream
2 cloves	garlic, pressed
1½ teaspoons	chili powder
1 teaspoon	salt
1 teaspoon	ground cumin
1 (4-ounce) can	diced chilies, drained
1½ cups	Monterey Jack cheese, shredded
1½ cups	green onions, thinly sliced
2 cups	cooked chicken, cubed
10	flour tortillas
1 cup	Cheddar cheese, shredded
2 cups	lettuce, shredded
1 cup	tomato, coarsely chopped
1 cup	Monterey Jack cheese, shredded
1 cup	guacamole
1 cup	salsa

Preheat oven to 375 degrees. Combine sour cream, garlic, chili powder, salt, cumin, chilies, 1½ cups of Monterey Jack cheese, green onion and chicken. Spoon about ½ cup of the mixture down the center of each tortilla. Roll up tortilla to enclose filling. Place tortillas seam-side down in a single layer in a shallow 3-quart baking dish. Cover and bake until hot, about 20 minutes. Remove cover and sprinkle evenly with Cheddar cheese. Return to oven and bake uncovered until cheese melts, about 3 to 5 minutes. Serve with lettuce, tomato, Monterey Jack cheese, guacamole and salsa.

Braised Chinese Chicken   *Serves 3–4*

1½ cups	soy sauce*
3 cups	water
5 slices	fresh ginger*
1 cup	brown sugar
1	star anise*
1 small	onion, sliced
¼ cup	sherry (optional)
3 pound	whole chicken fryer
	sesame oil*
1 head	won bok*, shredded
Garnish:	*Chopped green onions and chopped Chinese parsley*

Combine soy sauce, water, ginger, brown sugar, star anise, onion and sherry and bring to a boil. Immerse whole chicken in sauce. Bring sauce to a boil again. Reduce heat to medium and simmer one side of chicken for 25 minutes. Turn chicken and simmer an additional 25 minutes. Remove chicken from sauce, place on serving platter and let stand for 1 hour. Reserve sauce. Glaze chicken with a thin coat of sesame oil. Slice chicken and arrange on platter on a bed of shredded won bok. Heat ¾ cup sauce and pour it over the chicken. Garnish with green onions and Chinese parsley.

Spicy Eggplant with Chicken

Serves 4

An interesting combination of Asian flavors.

1 teaspoon	fresh ginger,* minced
3 tablespoons	soy sauce*
1 tablespoon	white vinegar
2 – 3 cloves	garlic, minced
1 tablespoon	sugar
2 – 3	fresh Hawaiian red chili peppers,* minced with seeds
1 teaspoon	cornstarch
½ – ¾ pounds	long eggplant, sliced diagonally in ½-inch pieces
¾ pound	ground chicken or turkey
	vegetable oil
Garnish:	*Chinese parsley**

Mix ginger, soy sauce, vinegar, garlic, sugar, chili pepper and cornstarch. Set aside. Sauté eggplant in oil in a large skillet until slices are slightly browned. Set aside. Sauté chicken until browned. Return eggplant to skillet and add sauce. Cook until thoroughly heated. Garnish with Chinese parsley.

Plantation
Cornish Game Hens

Serves 4–6

Game hens with a tropical twist.

4	**Cornish game hens**
	salt and freshly ground pepper
	to taste
2 tablespoons	**butter, melted**
1 (20-ounce) can	**pineapple* chunks packed in juice**
½ cup	**orange marmalade**
1 ½ tablespoons	**cornstarch**
2 tablespoons	**lemon juice**
1 tablespoon	**butter**
3	**firm bananas, cut into chunks**
2 tablespoons	**Cointreau**
Garnish:	*orange slices*

Preheat oven to 325 degrees. Cut hens in half lengthwise. Rinse and pat dry. Place hens, skin side up, in a greased shallow baking pan. Sprinkle with salt and pepper and brush with melted butter. Bake for 50 minutes. Drain pineapple chunks, reserving juice. Pour pineapple juice into a saucepan. Add the marmalade and cook over low heat, stirring until melted. Dissolve the cornstarch in lemon juice and add to marmalade mixture. Cook the sauce, stirring constantly, until thick and clear. Add butter, bananas, pineapple chunks and Cointreau. Spoon sauce over hens and bake for an additional 10 minutes. Garnish with orange slices.

Mochiko Chicken Wings   *Serves 10 – 12*

A favorite for tailgate parties.

2 tablespoons	flour
¾ cup	cornstarch
¾ cup	mochiko* flour
1½ teaspoons	sugar
1 tablespoon	salt
½ cup	soy sauce*
2	eggs, beaten
½ cup	green onion, chopped
1 tablespoon	fresh ginger,* grated
3 – 4 pounds	chicken wings
	vegetable oil

Mix flour, cornstarch, mochiko flour, sugar and salt.
Set aside. In another bowl, combine soy sauce, eggs, green
onion and ginger and add to dry ingredients. Add chicken wings.
Cover and marinate for 2 hours in the refrigerator. Bring to room
temperature before frying. Deep fry the chicken wings in
vegetable oil at 350 degrees until golden brown and crispy
all over. Drain and serve.

Chicken with Herbs and Mushrooms

Serves 6 – 8

1 pint	mushrooms, sliced
½ cup *plus* 1 tablespoon	butter, divided
2	chicken fryers, cut into quarters flour
½ cup	butter
¼ cup	olive oil*
1 small	onion, chopped
1	green bell pepper, chopped
1 teaspoon	rosemary
1 tablespoon	fresh thyme
2 tablespoons	fresh parsley
	salt and freshly ground pepper to taste
1 cup	sherry

Preheat oven to 350 degrees. Sauté mushrooms in 1 tablespoon butter in a medium frying pan. Set aside. Flour the chicken and brown well in ½ cup butter and olive oil. Place in a roasting pan, hollow side up. Into each hollow, place some onion, green pepper, mushrooms, rosemary, thyme, parsley, salt and pepper. Pour sherry over chicken, making sure each piece gets moistened. Cover tightly with foil. Bake until tender, about 40 to 50 minutes.

Chinatown Chicken

Serves 4

1	whole chicken
1 tablespoon	sesame oil*
4 tablespoons	light soy sauce*
1/8 teaspoon	salt
1 tablespoon	fresh ginger,* grated
1 1/2 cups	green onions, sliced on the diagonal in 1-inch pieces
1/3 cup	peanut oil*

Place chicken into a pot of boiling water. Bring water to a boil again and turn off heat. Cover pot and let stand for one hour. Remove chicken. Debone and remove skin. Cut into bite-sized strips. Mix sesame oil and soy sauce together. Pour over chicken. Sprinkle chicken with salt. Sprinkle with grated ginger and green onions. Prior to serving, heat peanut oil until very hot but not smoking. Pour hot oil over chicken. Serve with brown or white rice.

Spaghetti Sauce with
Turkey Meatballs
Serves 6

A lean alternative to traditional meatballs.

Spaghetti Sauce

1 cup	onion, chopped
1 cup	green bell pepper, coarsely chopped
½ cup	carrot, coarsely chopped
½ cup	celery, sliced
4 large	fresh tomatoes, peeled and chopped
1 (6-ounce) can	tomato paste
2 tablespoons	basil
1 teaspoon	oregano
1 teaspoon	pepper
½ teaspoon	sugar
1 clove	garlic, pressed
½ teaspoon	salt
1 recipe	Turkey Meatballs
12 ounces	pasta, cooked and drained

Prepare meatballs and set aside. In a large saucepan or Dutch oven, brown onion, green pepper, carrot and celery. Carefully stir in tomatoes, tomato paste, spices, sugar, garlic and salt. Bring to a boil and reduce heat. Add meatballs, cover and simmer for 30 minutes. If desired, uncover and simmer for 10 minutes or longer to thicken sauce. Adjust spices to taste. Serve over hot, cooked pasta.

Turkey Meatballs

1	egg, beaten
2 tablespoons	milk
¼ cup	fine dry bread crumbs
½ teaspoon	Italian seasoning
½ teaspoon	salt
½ teaspoon	pepper
1 pound	ground turkey

continued...

Preheat oven to 375 degrees. In a medium bowl, combine the egg, milk, bread crumbs and spices. Add turkey and mix well. Shape meat into 24 1-inch balls. Place meatballs into a lightly greased 13 x 9 x 2-inch baking pan Bake for 20 minutes or until center of meatball is no longer pink. Drain on paper towels.

Turkey Sausages

Serves 4 – 6

Sausages without guilt!

1 pound	**ground turkey**
1½ teaspoons	**sage**
¼ teaspoon	**thyme**
¼ teaspoon	**parsley**
¼ teaspoon	**cayenne**
½ teaspoon	**freshly ground pepper**
½ teaspoon	**garlic salt**
¼ teaspoon	**fennel seed**
1	**bay leaf**

Combine turkey, sage, thyme, parsley, cayenne, pepper, garlic salt and fennel. Mix well and form into 12 patties. Fry over medium heat in a non-stick skillet, adding the bay leaf to the pan. Cook until meat is well browned on both sides and no longer pink when slashed.

Chicken Siu Mai

Makes 24 pieces

*A steamed Chinese dumpling often served as dim sum.**

Dipping Sauce:

1 tablespoon	dry hot mustard
½ teaspoon	water
⅓ cup	soy sauce*

Mix dry mustard with water to form a thick paste. Let stand 15 minutes. Stir in soy sauce. Set aside.

4	shiitake mushrooms*
¼ cup	water chestnuts,* chopped
1 tablespoon	green onions, chopped
1 pound	boneless chicken breast, finely chopped
6 large	raw shrimp, cleaned and finely chopped
1¼ teaspoons	cornstarch
1½ teaspoons	sugar
¼ teaspoon	white pepper
1 tablespoon	sesame oil*
2 teaspoons	soy sauce*
1 tablespoon	oyster sauce*
1	egg, beaten
1 (8-ounce) package	won ton wrappers
	lettuce leaves

continued...

Soak mushrooms in water for about 30 minutes. Remove stems and discard. Finely chop remainder of mushrooms. Combine mushrooms with water chestnuts, green onions, chicken, shrimp, cornstarch, sugar, pepper, sesame oil, soy sauce, pepper and oyster sauce. Lightly brush beaten egg onto won ton wrapper. Place approximately 1 rounded tablespoon of filling in center of wrapper. Bring sides of wrapper up, creating a pouch and gently squeeze until filling reaches the top of the wrapper. Gently tap the siu mai on a cutting board or other flat surface to flatten the bottom. Repeat until filling is used up. Lightly grease steamer and line bottom with lettuce leaves. Place siu mai in steamer, leaving a ½-inch space between them. Place steamer over boiling water, cover and steam for 12 to 15 minutes. Serve with Dipping Sauce.

Crispy Cheddar Chicken   *Serves 4*

¾ cup	**dry bread crumbs**
½ cup	**Cheddar cheese, grated**
1 tablespoon	**parsley**
¼ teaspoon	**salt**
dash	**freshly ground pepper**
4	**boneless chicken breasts**
½ cup	**butter, melted**

Preheat oven to 375 degrees. Mix bread crumbs, Cheddar cheese, parsley, salt and pepper. Dip the chicken in the melted butter and then into the bread-crumb mixture. Place skin side up on a 9 x 9-inch baking dish. Sprinkle with remaining bread crumb mixture. Drizzle remaining butter over top. Bake for 20 – 25 minutes.

Baked Chicken Dijon

Serves 4

3 tablespoons	**fresh parsley, minced**
5 tablespoons	**Parmesan cheese,* freshly grated**
1½ cups	**panko* bread crumbs**
1 clove	**garlic, crushed**
½ cup	**butter or margarine**
6 teaspoons	**Dijon mustard***
4	**boneless chicken breasts, skinned**
Garnish:	*Freshly grated Parmesan cheese**

Combine parsley, Parmesan cheese and bread crumbs. Sauté garlic in butter until lightly browned. Stir in mustard. Remove from heat and cool slightly. Whip vigorously until mixture thickens. Dip chicken in mustard marinade until well coated. Then dip into bread-crumb mixture, packing crumbs onto chicken. Place breaded chicken into a lightly greased baking dish. Repeat for each chicken breast. Cover and refrigerate for several hours to set crumbs. Preheat oven to 350 degrees. Bake for 20 minutes, or until chicken is lightly browned. Top with grated Parmesan cheese.

Chicken Florentine

Serves 4

A colorful pasta dish with a hint of red pepper.

½ cup	butter
1 medium	onion, sliced
2 cloves	garlic, minced
1 tablespoon	basil
½ teaspoon	crushed red pepper
2½ pounds	chicken thighs
8 ounces	linguine
1 (10-ounce) package	frozen chopped spinach, thawed and squeezed dry
1 cup	Parmesan cheese,* grated
	salt and freshly ground pepper to taste
1 small	orange, quartered

Preheat oven to 400 degrees. Melt butter in a
10 x 15-inch roasting pan. Stir in onion, garlic, basil and red
pepper. Place chicken in the butter mixture, then turn over
to coat. Bake uncovered about 45 minutes. While chicken is
baking, cook linguine in boiling salted water and drain. Remove
chicken from pan and keep warm. Add spinach to pan and stir
to mix with drippings. Add linguine and cheese and toss.
Season to taste. Place a portion of the spinach and linguine
on individual serving plates. Flank with chicken. Garnish with
orange wedges to be squeezed over chicken and pasta.

Orange Chicken Almondine

1 cup	dry bread crumbs
¼ cup	almonds, finely chopped
1 teaspoon	salt
⅛ teaspoon	white pepper
2 tablespoons	fresh parsley, chopped
¼ cup	frozen orange juice concentrate, thawed
¼ cup	butter, melted
6	chicken breasts

Preheat oven to 350 degrees. Combine bread crumbs, almonds, salt, pepper and parsley. Combine orange juice concentrate and butter. Dip chicken breasts into orange juice and butter mixture and then into bread-crumb mixture. Bake in a shallow baking dish for 45 to 50 minutes.

Chicken Piccata

Serves 4

Lemon juice and capers add tartness to this savory chicken dish.

2	**whole chicken breasts, skinned, boned and halved**
½ cup	**flour**
½ teaspoon	**salt**
½ teaspoon	**freshly ground pepper**
½ teaspoon	**paprika**
2 tablespoons	**butter**
¼ cup	**olive oil***
4 tablespoons	**dry white wine**
2 tablespoons	**water**
3 tablespoons	**lemon juice**
1	**lemon, sliced**
3 – 4 tablespoons	**capers***
¼ cup	**parsley, minced**

Place chicken breasts between two sheets of waxed paper and gently pound until each is ¼-inch thick. Combine flour, salt, pepper and paprika. Dredge chicken in flour, shaking off any excess. Melt butter with oil in a large skillet. Sauté chicken on high heat until browned, about 2 to 3 minutes on each side. Drain and keep warm. Add wine and water to pan and bring to a boil. Scrape the bottom of pan to loosen any browned bits. Stir in lemon juice and cook until sauce thickens. Reduce the heat and add the chicken. Place lemon slices on top of the chicken. Add capers and sprinkle with parsley. Simmer gently until chicken is heated through. Serve over buttered pasta with sauce spooned on top.

Seared Shutome Medallions with Maui Onions and Kula Tomatoes

Serves 4

1 medium	Maui onion,* peeled and finely diced
2 tablespoons	butter
2	Kula tomatoes,* peeled, seeded and finely diced
1 sprig	fresh thyme
	salt and freshly ground pepper to taste
8 (3-ounce) slices	shutome,* cut ½-inch thick
4 tablespoons	virgin olive oil*
Garnish:	*8 small fresh thyme sprigs*

Sauté the onion in butter until tender. Add the tomatoes and thyme. Season and simmer over low heat for 3 minutes. Adjust seasoning and reserve. Season the shutome medallions and rub them with olive oil. Sear in a very hot pan for about 1½ minutes, leaving the fish underdone inside. Top each fish medallion with the onion and tomato mixture. Garnish with fresh thyme and serve.

Dominque Jamain
Kahala Hilton
Honolulu, Hawai'i

Poached Trout

Trout with a Southeast Asian twist.

1 – 2 pounds	**fresh whole trout**
	water to cover fish
1 tablespoon	**fresh ginger,* chopped**
2 tablespoons	**soy sauce***
2 tablespoons	**Chinese parsley,* chopped**
2 tablespoons	**green onions, chopped**
1 teaspoon	**fresh ginger,* grated**
1½ tablespoons	**peanut oil***

Clean fish. In a large deep skillet, bring the water and chopped ginger to a boil. Add fish and turn off heat. Let sit for 20 minutes. Put the fish on a platter and garnish with Chinese parsley, green onions and ginger. Heat peanut oil to smoking and pour over fish. Serve.

Kahuku Prawns

Serves 4

Prawns are grown commercially on O'ahu's North shore.

3 tablespoons	olive oil*
12	prawns, shelled (except tail), split and cleaned
¼ cup	butter
1 small clove	garlic, crushed
¼ teaspoon	salt
¼ teaspoon	freshly ground pepper
¼ cup	dry vermouth
3 tablespoons	lemon juice

Sauté prawns in olive oil on high heat until golden brown. Reduce heat and add butter, garlic, salt and pepper. Stir to blend. Transfer cooked prawns to a heated platter. To pan juices, add dry vermouth and lemon juice. Cook for one minute, stirring constantly and pour over prawns.

Broiled Tuna Steaks

¾ cup	olive oil*
	salt and freshly ground pepper to taste
1	bay leaf
½	onion, chopped
2	tuna steaks (2 – 2½ pounds)
2 cloves	garlic, chopped
2 tablespoons	parsley, chopped
2 tablespoons	capers,* chopped

Combine ½ cup olive oil, salt, pepper, bay leaf and onion. Marinate tuna in seasoned oil for 1 hour. Preheat the broiler. Remove the tuna from the marinade and place on a broiling rack that has been preheated for 10 minutes. Broil the fish 4 inches from heat, brushing the steaks occasionally with marinade. Cook evenly on both sides for about 10 minutes or until flesh is opaque. Combine remaining ¼ cup olive oil, garlic, parsley and capers and pour over top of fish. Serve immediately.

Swordfish with
Sweet and Sour Sauce

Serves 2

Serve with a green salad for a light summer supper.

2 (6-ounce)	**swordfish steaks**
	salt and freshly ground pepper
	to taste
	flour
2 tablespoons	**vegetable oil**
1 teaspoon	**flour**
6 tablespoons	**white wine**
¼ cup	**balsamic vinegar***
1½ tablespoons	**butter**
1 tablespoon	**capers,* drained**
2 teaspoons	**olive oil***
pinch	**sugar**
Garnish:	*Parsley sprigs*

Season fish with salt and pepper. Lightly dredge in flour and shake off excess. Heat vegetable oil in a heavy large skillet over medium high heat. Add fish and cook to desired degree of doneness, about four minutes per side for medium. Transfer to warm platter. Cover and keep warm. Pour off oil from skillet. Add one teaspoon flour to skillet and cook on high heat until brown, stirring constantly, about one minute. Add wine, vinegar, butter, capers, olive oil and sugar and cook, stirring frequently, until sauce is syrupy, about 8 minutes. Pour over fish, garnish and serve.

Dijon Tomato Fish Pouches

Serves 8

A different way to barbecue fish that leaves your grill clean!

8 (6-ounce)	fresh fish fillets, 'opakapaka* or onaga*
	salt and freshly ground pepper to taste
3 medium	shallots, minced
3 medium cloves	garlic, minced
¾ cup	vegetable oil
¼ cup	Dijon mustard*
2 tablespoons	fresh lemon juice
1 tablespoon	dried basil
1 pound	fresh plum tomatoes,* thinly sliced
2 tablespoons	fresh chives, snipped
Garnish:	*Fresh parsley*

Prepare barbecue. Cut pieces of foil large enough to wrap each serving of fish. Sprinkle fish with salt and pepper and set on foil. Combine shallots, garlic, oil, mustard, lemon juice and basil and mix well. Spread over fish. Cover each piece of fish with tomato slices and sprinkle with salt, pepper and chives. Wrap tightly, leaving space above fish for steam to collect. Place on grill and cook until fish is firm to the touch and no longer translucent, about 10 to 12 minutes. Remove foil, transfer to serving platter and garnish with parsley.

Heavenly Shrimp

½ cup	clam broth
½ cup	dry white wine (optional)
1 pound	medium to large shrimp, shelled and deveined
4 ounces	feta cheese,* crumbled
5	mushrooms, sliced
1 (14½-ounce) can	sliced or stewed tomatoes
½	red onion, diced
½	green bell pepper, diced

Bring clam broth to a boil in a skillet over medium heat. Add shrimp and cook until shrimp are cooked through, about 2 to 3 minutes. Stir in cheese, mushrooms, tomatoes, onion and bell pepper. Cook, stirring occasionally, until cheese is melted. Serve over rice.

Citrus Grilled Fish

Serves 6 – 8

½ cup	softened butter or margarine
2 to 3 tablespoons	fresh lime juice
1 teaspoon	lime peel, grated
dash	salt
3 – 4 pounds	fresh ahi,* aku,* or uku*
	oil
	salt and freshly ground pepper to taste
1 teaspoon	lemon peel, grated
1 or 2	limes, thinly sliced
1 or 2	lemons, thinly sliced
Garnish:	*Lime wedges*

Combine butter, lime juice, lime peel and salt in a small bowl. Beat until soft and light. Chill until ready to serve. Prepare barbecue. Clean fish. Rub fish with oil, inside and out. Season inside with pepper and lemon peel. Overlap alternating lime and lemon slices in cavity of fish. Place fish in an oiled fish basket or on a piece of oiled heavy-duty foil with several holes, or directly onto the oiled grill. Cover grill with lid or an aluminum foil tent and cook fish for 10 minutes for every inch of thickness. Turn fish and re-oil fish basket, foil or grill halfway through cooking time. Cut the lime butter into thin slices. Overlap slices on top of cooked fish. Garnish with lime wedges and serve.

Tofu Tuna Bake

Serves 6

A quick and easy meal.

20 ounces	**firm tofu,* well drained**
1 (6⅛-ounce) can	**water-packed tuna, drained**
½ cup	**water chestnuts,* chopped**
¾ cup	**green onions, chopped**
½	**carrot, grated**
4 ounces	**shiitake* mushrooms, chopped**
or	
1 (4-ounce) can	**mushroom stems and pieces**
½ cup	**mayonnaise**
2	**eggs, beaten**
2 tablespoons	**soy sauce***
1 tablespoon	**sugar**
½ teaspoon	**salt**
Garnish:	*Chopped parsley*

Preheat oven to 350 degrees. Combine all ingredients and pour into a lightly greased 8 x 8-inch baking pan. Bake uncovered for 35 minutes. Garnish and serve.

Shrimp and Dill Sandwich *Serves 6*

1 pound	**bay shrimp, cooked**
¾ cup	**mozzarella cheese, diced**
½ cup	**Monterey Jack or Swiss cheese, diced**
⅔ cup	**green onions, chopped**
½ cup	**mayonnaise**
2 teaspoons	**white vinegar**
1 teaspoon	**dill**
dash	**lemon juice**
	salt and freshly ground pepper
	to taste
6	**French rolls**

Combine first nine ingredients. Cover and chill for at least 45 minutes. Preheat oven to 400 degrees. Halve French rolls lengthwise. Mound shrimp mixture on top of bread and bake for 20 minutes or until cheese bubbles. Then broil until top is lightly browned.

Seared and Smoked Ahi with Pistachio Pesto, Ogo Wasabi Sauce and Radish Salsa

Serves 4

The condiments can be made ahead for this exotic entree.

1 (12-ounce) piece	**sashimi grade ahi,* cut into strips**
6 ounces	**Pistachio Pesto**
6 ounces	**Ogo Wasabi Sauce**
1 ½ cups	**Radish Salsa**
1 ounce	**olive oil***
Garnish:	*4 small bunches ogo* and 1/2 cup finely chopped Chinese parsley**

Brush ahi strips with pistachio pesto. Sear ahi in olive oil on all sides, keeping the fish raw in the center. Lightly smoke ahi for approximately 10 to 15 minutes. Cut into slices ¼-inch thick and lay across serving platter. Ladle wasabi sauce over one half of the fish slices and pesto over the other half. Spoon salsa in the middle of the platter. Garnish with ogo bunches and chopped Chinese parsley.

Pistachio Pesto

¼ cup	**pistachio nuts, lightly toasted in the oven**
3 cloves	**garlic, sautéed until light brown**
½ cup	**extra virgin olive oil***
½ cup	**Parmesan cheese,* grated**
¼ teaspoon	**freshly ground black pepper**
1 cup	**fresh basil, chopped**
	salt to taste

Puree all ingredients in a food processor.

continued...

Ogo Wasabi Sauce

½ teaspoon	Wasabi* paste
¼ teaspoon	dry mustard paste
1 teaspoon	Dijon mustard*
3 tablespoon	soy sauce*
4 tablespoons	plain yogurt
2 tablespoons	chopped dill
2 tablespoons	ogo,* finely chopped
1 teaspoon	inomona,* finely chopped (optional)

Mix all ingredients together.

Radish Salsa

3 tablespoons	red radish
2 tablespoons	daikon*
3 tablespoons	lychee*
2 tablespoons	jicama*
2 tablespoons	Maui onion*
2 tablespoons	cucumber
1 ounce	olive oil*
½ teaspoon	sesame oil*
1 tablespoon	Chinese parsley*
1 teaspoon	opal basil*
¾ ounce	lime juice
1 ounce	rice wine*
¼ teaspoon	chili pepper
	salt to taste

Dice radish, daikon, lychee, jicama, onion and cucumber into ⅛-inch pieces and combine in a stainless steel bowl. Add olive oil, sesame oil, Chinese parsley, opal basil, lime juice, rice wine, chili pepper and salt and mix well. Adjust seasoning and chill.

Sunset Sea Scallops

2 tablespoons	frozen orange juice concentrate, thawed
1 teaspoon	Dijon mustard*
	freshly ground black pepper
2 tablespoons	extra-virgin olive oil*
2 tablespoons	fresh basil, chopped
	salt to taste
2 tablespoons	olive oil*
1½ pounds	fresh scallops
1½ pounds	fresh spinach, washed, trimmed and torn in bite-size pieces
2 teaspoons	orange peel, finely grated

In a small bowl, whisk together orange juice, mustard and pepper. Slowly stir in olive oil. Add 1 tablespoon basil and season with salt. Set aside. Heat olive oil in a large skillet. Over medium heat, cook half of the scallops at a time for 4 to 5 minutes or until opaque and lightly browned. While scallops are cooking, steam the spinach in the moisture that clings to the leaves until tender, about 3 minutes. When scallops are done, drain the spinach and arrange on a large serving platter. Center the scallops on the spinach and pour orange dressing on top. Garnish with remaining basil and orange zest and serve immediately.

Herb Marinated Shrimp

Serves 4

¾ cup	**olive oil***
¾ cup	**sherry**
2 tablespoons	**parsley, minced**
1 tablespoon	**chives, minced**
1 teaspoon	**garlic, crushed**
1 teaspoon	**tarragon, minced**
	salt and freshly ground pepper to taste
2 pounds	**shrimp, peeled and deveined**

In a bowl, combine the olive oil, sherry, parsley, chives, garlic, tarragon, salt and pepper. Mix well. Add shrimp and toss. Cover and refrigerate for at least 4 hours, tossing every 30 minutes. Drain well. Place on a broiler pan and broil until lightly browned and just cooked.

Note: The shrimp can be marinated up to 24 hours ahead.

Cheri's Primo Shrimp

Serves 4

½ teaspoon	cayenne
1 teaspoon	freshly ground pepper
½ teaspoon	salt
½ teaspoon	dried thyme leaves
½ teaspoon	rosemary, crushed
½ teaspoon	oregano
½ clove	garlic, minced
1 teaspoon	Worcestershire sauce
½ cup	shrimp stock
½ cup	beer
1 pound	shrimp, peeled and deveined
9 tablespoons	sweet butter, melted

Combine cayenne, pepper, salt, thyme, rosemary, oregano, garlic, Worcestershire sauce, shrimp stock and beer. Add shrimp, cover, and refrigerate overnight. Skewer shrimp and barbecue 2 to 3 minutes per side. Melt butter and drizzle on top of cooked shrimp.

Shrimp Bake

Serves 4

1 cup	onion, chopped
1 clove	garlic, minced
½ cup	celery, chopped
¼ cup	butter
1 pound	fresh mushrooms, sliced
2 cups	cooked medium shrimp
2 cups	cooked rice
1 cup	green bell pepper, chopped
¼ cup	pimentos, drained and diced
2½ cups	tomatoes, drained
½ teaspoon	salt
¾ teaspoon	chili powder
¼ cup	butter, melted
Garnish:	*2 tablespoons fresh parsley, minced*

Preheat oven to 300 degrees. Grease a 2-quart casserole. Sauté onion, garlic and celery in ¼ cup butter until tender. Add mushrooms and sauté for 1 minute more. Blend in shrimp, rice, vegetables and seasonings. Pour mixture into casserole. Pour melted butter over the top. Bake uncovered for 45 – 50 minutes. Sprinkle with parsley before serving.

Coquilles Saint Jacques

Serves 2– 4

A lighter version of a classic seafood recipe.

1 pound	scallops, cut into ½-inch pieces
1 clove	garlic, pressed
4 teaspoons	olive oil,* divided
1 teaspoon	tarragon, finely chopped
1 tablespoon	parsley, finely chopped
2 tablespoons	scallions, finely chopped
1 tablespoon	flour
½ cup	skim milk
1 tablespoon	fresh Parmesan cheese,* grated
2 teaspoons	blue cheese, crumbled
2 tablespoons	white wine
	freshly ground pepper
½ cup	sliced mushrooms

Sauté scallops, garlic, tarragon, parsley and scallions in 2 teaspoons olive oil until vegetables are tender and scallops are opaque throughout. Set aside. In a large skillet, cook remaining olive oil and flour together over medium heat. Gradually stir in milk and cheeses, stirring continuously until smooth. Add wine, pepper, mushrooms and scallop mixture. Simmer two to three minutes. Serve with rice.

Mary's Baby Lamb Chops

Serves 8 – 10

This is excellent with Sweet Curry Pilaf.

16 – 24	lamb loin or rib chops, cut no more than ¾-inch thick

Marinade

½ cup	vegetable oil
¼ cup	soy sauce*
½ cup	red wine
1 teaspoon	fresh ginger,* grated
2 cloves	garlic, crushed
1½ teaspoons	curry powder
2 tablespoons	catsup
¼ teaspoon	freshly ground pepper
¼ teaspoon	Tabasco

Combine marinade ingredients and marinate lamb in refrigerator for 2 to 8 hours, turning occasionally. Broil for 2 minutes on each side. Baste lamb chops with marinade while broiling, if desired. Heat remaining marinade and spoon over the top of the lamb chops and serve.

Lamb and Goat Cheese Fettuccine

Serves 4 – 6

Pair this dish with Hearts of Palm Salad for an exotic dinner.

½ cup	olive oil*
½ pound	boneless lamb shoulder, trimmed of excess fat and cut into ¼ – ⅛-inch dice
4 cloves	garlic, minced
2 cups	lamb or beef stock
1 (28-ounce) can	Italian-style peeled tomatoes, drained and chopped
¾ pound	round eggplant, thinly sliced
½ teaspoon	salt
1 teaspoon	freshly ground pepper
1 pound	spinach fettucine or pappardelle
¼ pound	mild goat cheese, crumbled
¼ cup	Italian flat leaf parsley,* chopped

In a large saucepan, sauté lamb in ¼ cup of the oil until brown on all sides, about 2 minutes. Reduce the heat to medium and add the garlic. Cook, stirring until the garlic is fragrant but not brown, about 30 seconds. Add the stock and tomatoes. Reduce the heat and simmer, uncovered, for 1½ hours, stirring occasionally. In a large skillet, heat the remaining olive oil over high heat and sauté the eggplant slices, turning once, until browned, about 2 minutes per side. Add to the lamb sauce. Season with salt and pepper. In a large pot of boiling salted water, cook pasta until tender but still firm. Drain well. Return the pasta to the pot and toss with the hot lamb sauce. Add the goat cheese and toss again. Garnish with parsley and serve.

Four Peppercorn Pork Roast

Serves 8 – 10

4½ pound	boneless pork loin, tied
3 tablespoons	unsalted butter, softened
2 tablespoons	flour
¼ cup	mixed peppercorns, very coarsely crushed
¼ cup	flour
1¾ cups	chicken broth
1 cup	water
2 tablespoons	red wine vinegar*
	salt to taste
Garnish:	*Fresh rosemary*

Preheat oven to 475 degrees. Season roast with salt. Combine the butter and 2 tablespoons of flour to make a paste. Spread the top of the roast with the paste. Lightly press the peppercorns into the butter paste. Place the pork on a rack in a roasting pan. Roast at 475 degrees for 30 minutes. Reduce heat to 325 degrees and continue roasting for 1½ to 1⅔ hours or until meat thermometer registers 155 degrees. Transfer the roast to cutting board and let stand for 10 minutes. Prepare sauce while the roast is standing. Pour all but ¼ cup of fat from the roasting pan. Whisk in flour and cook over moderate heat for 3 minutes, stirring constantly. Slowly stir in the chicken broth and water. Bring to a boil. Stir in red wine vinegar and salt to taste. Simmer sauce until thickened to desired consistency. Remove string from roast and cut into ½-inch thick slices. Arrange on platter with sauce and garnish with fresh rosemary.

Pacific Island Grill

Serves 4

¼ cup	sesame seeds*
¼ cup	green onion, thinly sliced
3 tablespoons	soy sauce*
2 tablespoons	sesame* or salad oil
1 tablespoon	vinegar
1 tablespoon	brown sugar
1 tablespoon	fresh ginger*, minced
1 tablespoon	garlic, minced
1 teaspoon	dry mustard
1 teaspoon	Worcestershire sauce
1½ pounds	flank steak

In a medium skillet, stir sesame seeds over low heat until golden, about 2 to 3 minutes. Crush in a mortar and pestle, blender or food processor. Combine with green onions, soy sauce, oil, vinegar, brown sugar, ginger, garlic, mustard and Worcestershire. Place flank steak in a 9 x 13-inch baking pan and coat with marinade. Cover and chill, turning occasionally, for at least 4 hours or overnight. Grill the steak 4 inches above the hot coals, basting frequently with marinade, about 5 to 6 minutes on each side. Slice steak thinly on the diagonal and serve.

Grilled Marinated Leg of Lamb

Serves 8

5 – 7 pound	**leg of lamb, boned and butterflied**
12 cloves	**garlic, crushed**
1 cup	**honey**
1 cup	**soy sauce***
½ cup	**dry sherry**
	freshly ground pepper to taste

Combine garlic, honey, soy sauce, sherry and pepper. Place lamb in marinade for 12 hours or overnight, turning every 2 hours. Allow lamb to come to room temperature before grilling. Grill the lamb 4 inches above the hot coals, basting frequently with marinade, about 20 minutes on each side. Let meat stand for 5 minutes before slicing. Serve immediately.

Variation: Substitute 2 teaspoons fresh rosemary for the sherry. Sprinkle rosemary over the lamb before serving.

Cashew Pork

1 tablespoon	cornstarch
1 tablespoon	soy sauce*
1 tablespoon	dry sherry
¾ pound	boneless pork, cut into cubes
4 tablespoons	vegetable oil, divided
1 cup	roasted cashews
½ teaspoon	fresh ginger*, minced
1	carrot, sliced and blanched
½ cup	bamboo shoots*, diced
½ cup	snow peas*

Sauce

⅓ cup	chicken broth
1 tablespoon	vinegar
1 tablespoon	soy sauce*
1 tablespoon	hoisin sauce*
½ teaspoon	sugar
¼ teaspoon	sesame oil*
¼ teaspoon	salt

Combine sauce ingredients and set aside. Mix cornstarch, soy sauce, and sherry. Add pork and stir. Add 1½ teaspoons oil and let stand 15 minutes. Heat wok and add 1 tablespoon vegetable oil. When hot, add cashews and stir-fry until golden. Remove and set aside. Increase heat and add remaining vegetable oil and ginger. Stir-fry pork in two batches, cooking until meat is slightly browned, about 4 minutes. Add 1 tablespoon vegetable oil, if necessary, to cook the second batch. Remove meat. Stir-fry carrot, bamboo shoots, and snow peas for 1 minute, then return pork to wok. Add sauce and bring to a boil, stirring until sauce thickens.

Spicy Pork Tenderloins　*Serves 6*

A spicy-sweet alternative to pork chops.

1-inch piece	**fresh ginger*, peeled and minced**
1	**hot green chili pepper, minced**
¼ teaspoon	**red pepper flakes, crushed**
⅓ cup	**honey**
3 tablespoons	**soy sauce***
3 tablespoons	**sesame oil***
1½ pounds	**pork tenderloins**

Combine ginger, chili pepper, red pepper flakes, honey, soy sauce and sesame oil. Marinate pork in refrigerator for 5 to 6 hours, turning occasionally. Remove from marinade. Broil 6 inches from heat for 3 to 5 minutes on each side, basting frequently with marinade. Slice and serve.

Perfect Prime Rib　*Serves 10 – 12*

This no-fuss dish is perfect, particularly for parties.

5 – 6 pound	**3 rib roast – narrow end**
	Hawaiian or sea salt
	freshly ground pepper to taste

Preheat oven to 375 degrees. Rub meat with salt and sprinkle with pepper. Place meat fat side up in a shallow roasting pan. Bake for one hour. (This may be done the night before serving or in the morning before serving.) Turn off heat but do not open the oven door at any time until the meat is ready to serve. Regardless of the length of time meat has been in the oven, 40 minutes before serving, turn oven on again to 375 degrees and bake for 40 minutes. The coating will be brown and crisp and the roast will be pink, juicy and medium-rare all the way through.

Oven-Barbecued Spareribs   *Serves 6*

A staple of Island picnics.

3 – 4 pounds	pork spare ribs
¾ cup	brown sugar
½ cup	cider vinegar
¼ cup	soy sauce*
3 tablespoons	dry mustard
8 – 10 dashes	Tabasco
¾ teaspoon	garlic salt

Bring spareribs to a boil in salted water and cover. Reduce heat and simmer until meat is tender, approximately 1 hour. Preheat oven to 325 degrees. Combine brown sugar, vinegar, soy sauce, mustard, Tabasco and garlic salt and heat to boiling. Drain spareribs and arrange meaty sides up on rack in shallow roasting pan. Spread with marinade and roast, basting frequently, until done and glazed, about 1 hour.

Savory Lamb Kabobs

Serves 6

Serve on a bed of hot fluffy rice.

1 cup	vegetable oil
½ cup	lemon juice
1 teaspoon	salt
1 teaspoon	freshly ground pepper
2 cloves	garlic, crushed
2 large	bay leaves
1½ teaspoons	dried dill weed
or	
2 tablespoons	fresh dill weed, chopped
3 pounds	boneless leg or shoulder of lamb, trimmed and cut into 2-inch cubes
3 medium	firm tomatoes, cut into quarters
3 medium	green bell peppers, seeded and quartered
3 small	onions, quartered

In a large porcelain or glass bowl, combine oil, lemon juice, salt, pepper, garlic, bay leaves and dill. Make one or two small cuts in each lamb cube to prevent puckering during cooking. Add lamb cubes, and toss to coat with marinade. Cover and refrigerate for 8 hours or overnight, turning 2 or 3 times. Drain and reserve the marinade. Divide lamb and vegetables into 6 equal portions. Alternating vegetables and meat, thread onto 6 barbecue skewers. Place skewers on a rack in a large broiler pan. Brush with marinade and broil 4 inches from heat as follows:

5 – 10 minutes for rare
10 – 12 minutes for medium
15 minutes for well done

Turn the kabobs 2 or 3 times during the cooking process and brush frequently with marinade.

Ginger Beef with Raisin Sauce

Serves 4

Raisins and ginger provide an interesting flavor contrast.

1 pound	**beef tenderloin**
2 tablespoons	**flour**
1 teaspoon	**paprika**
1-inch piece	**fresh ginger*, grated**
2 cloves	**garlic, crushed**
3 tablespoons	**vegetable oil**
⅓ cup	**raisins**
2 tablespoons	**butter**
1 teaspoon	**soy sauce***
3 tablespoons	**catsup**
½ cup	**water**

Slice beef across grain into thin strips. Dredge in flour mixed with paprika. Sauté ginger, garlic and beef in oil until meat is browned. Remove meat from pan. Stir in raisins, butter, soy sauce, catsup and water and bring to a boil. Add steak strips and simmer for 3 to 5 minutes. Serve over rice.

Hawaiian Barbecued Lamb

Serves 4 – 6

The crushed pineapple in the marinade adds a tropical touch.

2	large onions, minced
½ clove	garlic
2 tablespoons	butter
1 (20-ounce) can	crushed pineapple*, drained
¼ cup	brown sugar
1 tablespoon	salt
2 tablespoons	curry powder
3 tablespoons	vinegar
dash	cayenne
3 pounds	lamb, cut into 1-inch chunks
2	large onions, cut in chunks

Brown onions and garlic in butter. Add pineapple, sugar, salt, curry, vinegar and cayenne pepper. Pour into a large bowl. Add cubed lamb. Cover and refrigerate overnight, turning 2 or 3 times. Drain and reserve marinade. Thread meat and onions onto barbecue skewers. Grill over charcoal to desired degree of doneness or broil for 10 minutes, turning once. Heat reserved marinade and serve with meat.

Veal Marsala

Serves 1

7 ounces	**beef broth**
4 (1-ounce)	**boneless veal cutlets**
	flour
¼ cup	**mushrooms, sliced**
2 ounces	**butter**
1 ounce	**Marsala wine**
	salt and freshly ground pepper to taste
6 ounces	**pasta, cooked**
Garnish:	*Chopped parsley*

Cook beef broth over medium-high heat until reduced by half, stirring constantly. Set aside. Place the veal between two pieces of waxed paper and flatten each cutlet with the flat side of a mallet until thin. Dust lightly in flour. Sauté in butter until slightly browned on all sides. Remove veal. Add the mushrooms and sauté for 1 minute. Add wine and simmer for 1 minute. Add beef broth, salt and pepper and simmer for 1 minute more. Return veal to pan and cook until heated through. Place veal on top of pasta. Spoon sauce over veal and garnish with chopped parsley.

Juicy Meatloaf

A tried and true family dish.

2 pounds	**lean ground beef**
1	**egg**
1 cup	**carrots, grated**
1 cup	**potatoes, grated**
½ cup	**cooked white rice**
¼ cup	**onions, chopped**
2 tablespoons	**steak sauce**
2 teaspoons	**salt**
1 teaspoon	**freshly ground pepper**
1 (8-ounce) can	**tomato sauce**

Preheat oven to 350 degrees. Combine ground beef, egg, carrots, potatoes, rice, onions, steak sauce, salt and pepper and mix well. Place meat mixture in a 9 x 5 x 3-inch loaf pan and spread tomato sauce over it. Bake for 45 to 60 minutes or until meat in center is no longer pink when slashed. Cut into 1-inch slices.

Note: Ground turkey may be substituted for ground beef for a low-fat meatloaf.

Eggplant Parmesan

Serves 8 – 10

3 – 4	large round eggplants, peeled and cut into ¼ to ½-inch rounds
4 teaspoons	salt
1	egg
1 cup	milk
⅛ teaspoon	garlic powder
½ teaspoon	parsley
½ teaspoon	basil
½ teaspoon	salt
⅛ teaspoon	white pepper
	olive oil*
	flour
3 cups	Marinara Sauce
1½ pounds	mozzarella cheese, thinly sliced
½ cup	Parmesan cheese,* grated
½ cup	Romano cheese,* grated

Marinara Sauce

2 tablespoons	olive oil*
½ cup	carrot, minced
½ cup	celery minced
½ cup	onion, minced
2 – 3 cloves	garlic, crushed
1 (28-ounce) can	tomato puree
1 teaspoon	oregano
1 teaspoon	basil
2 – 3	bay leaves
¼ cup	beef broth
1⅔ cups	water
4 teaspoons	sugar
½ teaspoon	Worcestershire sauce
	salt and white pepper to taste

continued...

To prepare marinara sauce, sauté carrots, celery, onion and garlic in olive oil until tender, about 10 minutes. Stir in all other ingredients and season with salt and pepper. Simmer uncovered 25 minutes. Lay the eggplant slices on paper towels and sprinkle with salt. Let stand for 30 minutes. Preheat oven to 375 degrees. Shake or wipe any excess liquid off the eggplant slices. Beat egg with milk and add spices. In a medium skillet, heat small amount of olive oil. Flour each slice of eggplant, dip in egg mixture and brown on both sides. Set aside. In a 9 x 11 or 14 x 11-inch baking dish place 1 cup marinara sauce, then ⅓ of the eggplant slices and ⅓ of the mozzarella slices. Sprinkle with ⅓ of the Parmesan and Romano cheeses. Repeat twice. Bake uncovered for 20 minutes. Remove from oven and cover with foil. Bake an additional 10 minutes.

Cheesy Italian Vegetables

6 – 8 Servings

1 medium	cauliflower, cut into florets
2 large	tomatoes, cut into wedges
1 cup	Swiss cheese, grated
⅓ cup	butter or margarine, melted
¾ cup	Italian-seasoned bread crumbs
½ teaspoon	salt

Preheat oven to 375 degrees. Cook the cauliflower until just tender, about 6 minutes. Drain. Arrange cauliflower and tomatoes in a shallow 2-quart casserole. Sprinkle with cheese. Combine melted butter, bread crumbs and salt. Sprinkle bread crumb mixture over casserole. Bake for 20 minutes.

Szechuan Tofu

4 tablespoons	vegetable oil
6 cloves	garlic, minced
1½ pounds	round eggplant, cut into 1-inch cubes
⅓ cup	soy sauce*
3 tablespoons	white wine vinegar*
2 teaspoons	sugar
1 cup	water
2 cups	green onions, cut into 1-inch pieces
½ teaspoon	cayenne
20 ounces	firm tofu,* cut into 1-inch cubes

Heat oil and sauté the garlic until lightly browned. Add eggplant, water, soy sauce, vinegar, sugar and bring to a boil. Cover and cook until almost tender, about 6 minutes. Add the green onions and cayenne and simmer for 3 more minutes. Gently stir in tofu. Serve with rice.

Chilies Rellenos

¾ pound	**Monterey Jack cheese**
6	**fresh long green chilies, peeled and seeded**
	flour
8	**eggs, separated**
½ teaspoon	**salt**
	vegetable oil
Garnish:	*Salsa*

Cut Monterey Jack cheese into 6 long pieces and insert one into each chili. Roll lightly in flour. Beat egg whites until stiff but not dry. Beat yolks with salt and gradually fold into whites. Heat ¼ inch of oil in large frying pan. Spoon some egg mixture into oil, place a chili on the egg, then cover with more egg. Fry for 3 minutes and then carefully turn and fry other side until egg is set. Drain. Serve with salsa.

To peel and seed chilies, roast under a broiler until blackened on all sides. Place in a paper bag and close tightly. Steam chilies in bag for 15 to 20 minutes. Remove from bag and peel off skin. Cut a small slit in one side of chili and remove seeds and veins.

Nordic Super Sandwich   *Makes 2 cups*

Serve with pita bread.

20 ounces	**tofu*, rinsed, drained and cut into small squares**
¼ cup	**celery, sliced**
¼ cup	**green onions, sliced**
1 small	**carrot, shredded**
⅓ cup	**plain nonfat yogurt**
2 tablespoons	**mayonnaise**
2 teaspoons	**Dijon mustard***
	salt and freshly ground pepper

Combine tofu, celery, green onions, carrot, yogurt, mayonnaise, mustard, salt and pepper. Cover and chill for at least two hours to blend flavors.

To drain tofu, place pieces in a colander for ½ hour.

Cheddar Veggie Bake

Serves 4 – 6

1⅓ cups	**vegetable broth**
2 medium	**carrots, thinly sliced**
1 (8¾-ounce) can	**kidney beans, drained**
½ cup	**quick-cooking barley**
¼ cup	**green onions, chopped**
¼ cup	**parsley, chopped**
3 tablespoons	**bulgur wheat**
¼ cup	**water chestnuts, chopped**
¼ teaspoon	**salt**
⅛ teaspoon	**freshly ground pepper**
¼ teaspoon	**garlic powder**
2	**green onions, chopped**
½ cup	**sharp cheddar cheese, shredded**
Garnish:	*Chopped parsley*

Preheat oven to 350 degrees. Combine all ingredients except the cheese in a 1-quart casserole. Cover and bake for 50 minutes or until the barley and carrots are tender. Remove from oven and sprinkle the cheddar cheese over the casserole. Bake for 2 to 3 more minutes or until cheese is melted.

Ratatouille

Serves 6 – 8

This tastes great served over angel hair pasta.

1½ pounds	zucchini, cut into 2-inch lengths
1¼ pounds	eggplant, cubed
2 teaspoons	salt
2 large	onions, diced
1	green bell pepper, seeded and diced
1 cup	fresh Chinese parsley,* minced
2 large cloves	garlic, minced
2 medium	tomatoes, coarsely chopped
¼ cup	olive oil*
1 teaspoon	ground coriander
1 teaspoon	crushed thyme
1½ teaspoons	dried basil
3 rounded tablespoons	tomato paste
¼ cup	tomato sauce
	salt and pepper to taste
1 – 1½ teaspoons	sugar
Garnish:	*Chopped Chinese parsley**

Preheat oven to 350 degrees. Place zucchini and eggplant in colander. Sprinkle with 2 teaspoons salt and drain for 30 minutes. Pat vegetables dry with paper towels. In a large pot, sauté onion and pepper in olive oil for 3 minutes. Add eggplant and zucchini. Cover and let steam on medium heat for 10 minutes. Stir in Chinese parsley, garlic, tomatoes, coriander, thyme, basil, tomato paste, and tomato sauce. Simmer 10 minutes, uncovered. Add salt, pepper and sugar to taste. Transfer to an ovenproof casserole, cover and bake until soft, about 40 minutes. Garnish with Chinese parsley. Serve at room temperature or cold.

Creamy
Ratatouille Spread

Makes 2 cups

A tasty way to use leftover ratatouille.

¾ cup	**fresh Chinese parsley* leaves, loosely packed**
1 small *or*	
½ medium	**onion, quartered**
1 small clove	**garlic**
1 cup	**ratatouille, drained**
¾ cup	**pitted black olives**
1 cup	**sour cream**
1 teaspoon	**fresh lemon juice**
¼ teaspoon	**salt**

In a food processor, chop Chinese parsley, onion and garlic for 5 seconds. Scrape bowl. Add ratatouille, olives, sour cream, lemon juice and salt and process another 30 seconds, stopping to scrape the bowl once. Serve on warm pita bread, crackers, crudités or tomatoes or as a topping for hamburgers.

No-Egg Artichoke Quiche *Serves 6 – 8*

1 (6-ounce) jar	marinated artichoke hearts, chopped
1 cup	egg substitute
¼ cup	flour
½ teaspoon	baking powder
¼ teaspoon	freshly ground pepper
1 cup	low-fat ricotta cheese
2½ cups	low-fat Monterey Jack cheese, shredded

Preheat oven to 350 degrees. Drain artichoke hearts, reserving the marinade. Cut the artichokes into ½-inch pieces. Combine marinade with egg substitute, flour, baking powder and pepper. Beat with a rotary beater until blended. Stir in the ricotta cheese, 2 cups of the Monterey Jack cheese and the artichoke pieces. Pour mixture into a greased 9-inch round cake pan. Sprinkle remaining Monterey Jack cheese on top. Bake until top is lightly browned and center feels firm when gently touched, about 40 minutes. Cool to room temperature and cut into wedges. Serve or cover and chill to serve cold.

Spinach and
Feta Cheese Quiche

Serves 8

1 (9-inch)	deep dish pie shell, baked
1 (10-ounce) package	frozen chopped spinach, thawed
4	eggs, beaten
¾ cup	cream
1¼ cups	milk
¼ teaspoon	freshly ground pepper
2 tablespoons	lemon juice
2 tablespoons	parsley, chopped
¼ pound	feta cheese,* crumbled
3 tablespoons	Romano cheese,* freshly grated

Preheat oven to 375 degrees. Drain spinach and squeeze out as much water as possible. Beat eggs, cream, and milk. Add pepper, lemon juice and parsley. Stir in spinach and feta cheese. Pour mixture into baked crust. Sprinkle Romano cheese on top of quiche. Bake for 30-40 minutes or until a knife inserted in center comes out dry. Cool for 10 minutes before serving.

Armenian Vegetable Stew   *Serves 4*

A full-bodied vegetable stew that may be served hot or cold.

1 large	onion, chopped
5 tablespoons	olive oil,* divided
4 stalks	celery, cut into 1-inch pieces
2 cups	green beans, cut into 2-inch pieces
1 (28-ounce) can	whole tomatoes, including juice, coarsely chopped
or 4 cups	freshly chopped tomatoes
plus	1 cup tomato juice
3	bay leaves
3 large cloves	garlic, pressed
2 tablespoons	fresh basil, finely chopped
or 2 teaspoons	dried basil
½ teaspoon	ground thyme
1 medium	round eggplant
or 3 small	long eggplants, cut into ¾-inch pieces
	salt and freshly ground pepper
1½ tablespoons	lemon juice
Garnish:	*Lemon slices*

In a large pot, sauté onions in 3 tablespoons of olive oil over medium heat until onions are translucent. Add celery, stir, cover and cook for 5 minutes. Add green beans, tomatoes, bay leaves, garlic, basil and thyme, stir, cover and cook for 7 minutes. Place eggplant on top of the vegetables. Sprinkle with salt and pepper and drizzle with 2 tablespoons of olive oil. Cover and simmer for 20 minutes. Stir occasionally but do not let the eggplant touch the bottom of the pan and burn. After eggplant has released its juices, stir it in and continue simmering until eggplant and vegetables are tender. Stir in lemon juice. Garnish with lemon slices.

Papaya Indonesian

Serves 6

Serve with a light green salad for a colorful luncheon.

3 small or medium	papayas,* cut in half and seeded
1½ cups	small curd cottage cheese
1½ cups	cream cheese, softened
1 teaspoon	curry powder
2 tablespoons	chutney*
2 tablespoons	raisins
½ cup	water chestnuts,* slivered or diced
½ teaspoon	cinnamon
¼ cup	sugar
¼ cup	butter, melted

Preheat oven to 450 degrees. Blend cottage cheese, cream cheese, curry powder and chutney. Add the raisins and water chestnuts. Fill the papayas with the cheese mixture and place in a shallow baking dish. Mix the cinnamon and sugar together and sprinkle on the papayas. Pour melted butter over the top and bake for 15 minutes.

Vegetarian Chili
with Pink Onion Relish

Serves 6 – 8

1 small	green bell pepper, chopped
1 small	red bell pepper, chopped
⅓ cup	celery, chopped
2 large	onions, chopped
3 tablespoons	vegetable oil
1 tablespoon	mustard seed
2 tablespoons	chili powder
1 teaspoon	cumin seed
1 teaspoon	unsweetened cocoa
1 teaspoon	oregano
¼ teaspoon	cinnamon
1 (14½-ounce) can	whole tomatoes, including juice, broken into large chunks
3 (8¾-ounce) cans	kidney beans, with juice
1 (6-ounce) can	tomato paste
1 cup	water
	salt and pepper to taste
	Pink Onion Relish
Garnish:	*Grated cheddar cheese, sliced green peppers, chopped cucumbers and chopped tomatoes*

Sauté peppers, celery and onions in oil in a medium-sized saucepan until onions are golden brown and peppers are barely tender. Add mustard seed and cook for 1 minute, stirring constantly. Add chili powder, cumin seed, oregano, cinnamon, tomatoes, kidney beans, tomato paste, water, salt and pepper. Simmer for 40 minutes or until thickened, stirring occasionally. Garnish and serve.

continued...

Pink Onion Relish

2 cups	water
1½ teaspoons	white vinegar
1 large	red onion, thinly sliced
1½ teaspoons	vinegar
1 tablespoon	salad oil
½ teaspoon	mustard seed
¼ teaspoon	cumin seed
	salt to taste

Bring water and vinegar to a boil in a small saucepan. Add the red onion and boil 2 to 3 minutes. Make sure the onions are immersed in the liquid. Drain and cool onions. Mix the cooled onions with the vinegar, salad oil, mustard seed, cumin seed and salt. Serve with Vegetarian Chili.

Haku leis date back to ancient Hawai'i.
The leimakers braid flowers, leaves and even
fruits together, often weaving them into
a backing of ferns, ti or banana leaves.

Vegetables

Zucchini-Tomato Parmesan

Serves 8

3 large	zucchini, cut into ¼-inch slices
1 cup	onion, chopped
2 tablespoons	olive oil*
1 (28-ounce) can	Italian-style peeled tomatoes, drained and chopped
2 teaspoons	salt
1 teaspoon	freshly ground pepper
4 teaspoons	oregano
2 tablespoons	vinegar
½ cup	fresh Parmesan cheese,* grated

Preheat oven to 400 degrees. Arrange zucchini slices in a buttered casserole. Sauté onion in olive oil. Add tomatoes, seasonings and vinegar to the onions and bring to a boil. Simmer tomato-onion mixture for 1 minute. Pour over zucchini and sprinkle cheese on top. Bake uncovered for 45 minutes or until zucchini is tender.

Mexicali Eggplant

Even non-eggplant people love this spicy delicious dish!

1½ pounds	**eggplant, cut crosswise into ½-inch-thick rounds**
1 cup	**tomato sauce**
1 cup	**canned tomatoes, crushed**
¼ cup	**green onions, sliced**
¼ cup	**canned mild green chilies, drained and chopped**
8	**black olives, sliced**
2 cloves	**garlic, minced**
½ teaspoon	**ground cumin**
8 ounces	**Monterey Jack cheese, shredded**

Preheat oven to 450 degrees. On a lightly greased baking sheet, bake eggplant slices in a single layer for about 20 minutes. While eggplant is baking, combine the tomato sauce, crushed tomatoes, green onions, chilies, olives, garlic and cumin in a saucepan. Bring to a boil and simmer for 10 minutes. Line the bottom of a 1½-quart casserole with a single layer of eggplant slices followed by half of the tomato mixture and half of the cheese. Repeat layers ending with cheese. Bake at 350 degrees for about 25 minutes.

Stuffed Zucchini

2 large	**zucchini**
½	**onion, chopped**
1 tablespoon	**butter**
1 pound	**tomatoes, peeled, seeded and coarsely chopped**
1 clove	**garlic, minced**
1 teaspoon	**oregano**
	salt and freshly ground pepper to taste
1 tablespoon	**buttered bread crumbs**
Garnish:	*Grated Parmesan cheese* *****

Preheat oven to 325 degrees. Trim the ends of the zucchini, slice length-wise and hollow out, leaving a slight bottom to hold the filling. Reserve the zucchini pulp. Cook zucchini shells in boiling salted water until barely tender. Drain. Sauté the onion in butter. Add zucchini pulp, tomatoes, garlic, oregano, salt and pepper and cook, gently stirring, until the mixture becomes thick. Fill the zucchini shells with the tomato-zucchini mixture and place in a shallow baking pan. Sprinkle with bread crumbs. Cover and bake for 10 to 15 minutes or until heated through. Garnish with freshly grated Parmesan cheese.

Red Cabbage

Serves 4 – 6

Better than sauerkraut!

1 tablespoon	vegetable oil
1	onion, chopped
1 large	head red cabbage, coarsely chopped
1 large	tart apple, peeled and coarsely chopped
⅓ cup	vinegar
1 teaspoon	salt
3 tablespoons	sugar
¼ teaspoon	ground cloves
3	bay leaves

Combine ingredients in a large saucepan. Cover and simmer, stirring occasionally, for 1 hour or until cabbage is wilted and flavors are well blended.

Broccoli Elégante

Serves 4

6 slices	bacon, diced
¼ cup	scallions, chopped
¾ cup	walnuts, coarsely chopped
1 pound	broccoli, rinsed and trimmed

In a large skillet, cook bacon pieces over medium heat until crisp. Drain. Add scallions to the skillet and cook for 2 minutes. Add walnuts and cook, stirring frequently, for 5 minutes or until walnuts are golden. Return bacon to the pan and keep warm. In a large saucepan, cook broccoli in boiling salted water until tender, about 10 to 12 minutes. Drain. Top with the walnut mixture and serve.

Nuts Over Asparagus

Serves 4 – 6

1 pound	**fresh thin asparagus**
¼ cup	**salted cashew nuts**
4 tablespoons	**butter, divided**
2 tablespoons	**water**

Trim ends from asparagus and set aside. In a large heavy saucepan, stir-fry cashews in 2 tablespoons of butter over moderate heat for 2 minutes. Transfer cashews to paper towels to drain. Add the remaining butter to the pan and melt. Add the asparagus and cook on high heat for 1 minute. Reduce heat, add water, and simmer the asparagus, covered, for 3 to 4 minutes, or until it is tender but still crisp. Transfer the asparagus to a heated serving dish. Sprinkle with nuts. Serve.

Hofbrau Carrots

Serves 4

4 large	**carrots, peeled and julienned**
1 tablespoon	**butter**
¾ cup	**beer**
¼ cup	**chicken broth**
1 teaspoon	**dried dill weed**
¼ teaspoon	**salt**
1 teaspoon	**sugar**

Sauté carrots in butter over medium heat for 3 minutes. Add beer, chicken broth and dill. Cover and simmer, stirring often, until the carrots are tender but still crisp, about 10 minutes. Add the salt and sugar and cook, uncovered, for 3 minutes. Drain and serve.

Sweet Potato Casserole

Serves 6 – 8

The coconut adds a tropical twist to an old favorite.

4 cups	**sweet potatoes, cooked and mashed**
or	
2 (24-ounce) cans	**sweet potatoes or yams, drained**
2 tablespoons	**sugar**
⅓ cup	**butter**
½ cup	**milk**
, 2	**eggs, beaten**
⅓ cup	**flaked coconut***
⅓ cup	**pecans, chopped**
⅓ cup	**brown sugar**
2 tablespoons	**butter, melted**

Preheat oven to 325 degrees. Beat sweet potatoes, sugar, butter, milk, and eggs until light and fluffy. Pour into a 2-quart casserole. Mix coconut, pecans, brown sugar and melted butter and sprinkle on top of the sweet potatoes. Bake at 325 degrees for 1 hour or until potatoes are heated through and top is crunchy.

Sherried Kula Onions

Serves 4

¼ cup	butter
5	medium Kula or Maui onions,* thinly sliced
or	
3 large	onions, thinly sliced
½ teaspoon	sugar
½ teaspoon	salt
½ teaspoon	freshly ground pepper
½ cup	sherry
¼ cup	fresh Parmesan cheese,* grated
dash	nutmeg

Melt butter in a medium skillet over medium heat. Add onions, sugar, salt, and pepper. Cook over low heat until soft, about 5 to 8 minutes. Increase heat, add sherry and cook for 2 to 3 minutes. Sprinkle with Parmesan cheese and nutmeg and serve.

Savory Potatoes

Serves 4

Try this with broiled fish or baked ham.

2 pounds	small new potatoes, scrubbed
¼ cup	butter
1 tablespoon	olive oil*
	zest of 1 lemon, grated
¼ cup	fresh parsley, chopped
2 tablespoons	fresh chives, chopped
⅛ teaspoon	ground nutmeg
¼ teaspoon	salt
¼ teaspoon	freshly ground pepper
3 tablespoons	fresh lemon juice

Place potatoes in a large saucepan. Cover with water and bring to a boil over medium heat. Let boil for 15 – 20 minutes or until potatoes are fork-tender. Drain well. Set aside and keep warm. In a small saucepan over low heat, melt the butter and oil. Stir in lemon rind, parsley, chives, nutmeg, salt and pepper. Cook over low heat, stirring constantly, until steaming but do not allow the mixture to boil. Stir in lemon juice and pour over the warm potatoes. Toss gently to coat evenly. Serve at once.

Cut lemon zest with a vegetable peeler or a citrus zester. A hand grater may also be used. Be careful to use only the colored portion of the skin as the white pith beneath is bitter.

Broccoli Soufflé

Serves 6

4	**eggs, separated**
½ cup	**mayonnaise**
¼ cup	**flour**
1½ cups	**milk**
3 ounces	**Parmesan cheese,* grated**
1 (10-ounce) package	**frozen chopped broccoli, thawed and drained**

Preheat oven to 300 degrees. Combine the mayonnaise and flour in a medium saucepan over low heat. Gradually add milk, stirring constantly until mixture is thick and bubbly. Stir in cheese until melted. Remove from heat. Beat egg whites until stiff but not dry. Lightly beat egg yolks and add to cheese mixture. Stir in broccoli. Fold broccoli-cheese mixture into egg whites and pour into 1½-quart casserole. With the tip of a spoon make a slight indentation around the top of soufflé to form a top hat. Bake for 1 hour and 15 minutes. Serve immediately.

Eggs separate more easily when cold but beat to a higher volume faster at room temperature.

Hawaiian Sweet Potatoes   *Serves 6 – 8*

The grated potato gives this dish an unusual texture.

2	eggs
2 teaspoons	vanilla
2 cups	sweet potato, grated
1½ cups	evaporated milk
½ cup	sugar
¼ teaspoon	salt
½ cup	butter, melted
1 cup	coconut,* flaked

Preheat oven to 325 degrees. Beat eggs and vanilla. Add sweet potatoes, milk, sugar, salt, butter and coconut. Mix until well blended. Pour into a greased 10 x 7 x 2-inch baking dish and bake for 35 to 45 minutes or until custard is set.

Zucchini and Hominy   *Serves 5 – 6*

Perfect with grilled chicken.

2 tablespoons	butter
2 tablespoons	vegetable oil
1 small	onion, chopped
3 medium	zucchini, cut into ½-inch pieces
1 (14½-ounce) can	hominy, drained
2	tomatoes, chopped
2 tablespoons	lime juice
1 tablespoon	chili powder
1 teaspoon	salt
dash	freshly ground pepper

Melt butter with oil in a large skillet over medium heat. Stir in vegetables and seasonings. Cook, stirring occasionally, until zucchini is tender, about 10 to 15 minutes.

Cozy Butternut Squash

Serves 4 – 6

A comforting dish for a cold winter day.

4 pounds	**butternut squash, peeled, seeded and cut into 2-inch cubes**
1 (14½-ounce) can	**chicken broth**
2 cups	**water**
6 tablespoons	**butter, softened**
½ teaspoon	**ginger**
¼ teaspoon	**mace**
¼ teaspoon	**ground coriander**
½ teaspoon	**salt**
¼ teaspoon	**freshly ground white pepper**
pinch	**cayenne**
1 – 2 tablespoons	**fresh lemon juice**
2 tablespoons	**whipping cream**
Garnish:	*Pecan halves*

Preheat oven in 350 degrees. In large pot, boil squash in water and chicken broth for 20 minutes or until tender. Drain liquid and add butter, seasonings and lemon juice. Place in a blender or food processor and blend or process just until smooth. Transfer to a casserole dish and fold in the cream. Cover and bake for 25 minutes. Garnish with pecan halves and serve.

Ualakaa Yams

The nuts and raisins add texture to this dish.

6	**yams or sweet potatoes, cooked and mashed**
½ cup	**butter, melted**
½ cup	**light brown sugar**
1 teaspoon	**salt**
½ teaspoon	**nutmeg**
¾ teaspoon	**cinnamon**
½ cup	**half and half**
¾ cup	**pecans, chopped**
½ cup	**raisins**

Preheat oven to 350 degrees. Beat yams, butter, sugar and seasonings until light and fluffy. Stir in half and half, pecans and raisins. Bake in an 8-inch square pan for 30 minutes.

Note: For an impressive presentation, serve this in hollowed-out butternut squash or orange halves.

Tomato Wedges Provencale

Serves 6 – 8

4 large	tomatoes, cut into 8 wedges
3 tablespoons	butter or margarine, melted
3 tablespoons	Italian-seasoned bread crumbs
¼ cup	green onions, chopped
¼ cup	fresh parsley, chopped
2 cloves	garlic, minced
1 teaspoon	dried basil
	salt and freshly ground pepper to taste

Preheat oven to 425 degrees. Arrange tomato wedges in a single layer in buttered baking dish. Combine butter, bread crumbs, green onions, parsley, garlic, butter, basil, salt and pepper. Sprinkle bread-crumb mixture evenly over tomatoes. Bake uncovered for 12 to 15 minutes. Serve hot.

Eggplant with Miso Sauce

Serves 4

1 pound	**long Japanese eggplant,* cut into 1-inch slices**
4 tablespoons	**water, divided**
3 tablespoons	**white miso***
2 teaspoons	**sugar**
1 teaspoon	**mirin***
1 teaspoon	**sesame oil***
½ teaspoon	**fresh ginger,* grated**
1 tablespoon	**vegetable oil**
Garnish:	*1½ teaspoons toasted sesame seeds and 2 green onions, chopped*

Place eggplant on a plate with 1 tablespoon water and cover with plastic wrap. Microwave on high for 3 to 4 minutes or until eggplant is soft enough to pierce with a fork but not mushy. Drain and set aside. Mix miso with sugar and blend well. Blend in water, mirin, sesame oil, and ginger. In a skillet over medium heat, cook eggplant in vegetable oil until lightly browned. Add sauce and simmer, uncovered, until eggplant is tender, about 3 to 5 minutes. Garnish with toasted sesame seeds and chopped green onion and serve.

To toast sesame seeds, cook them in a skillet over medium heat until they are lightly colored.

Vegetable Curry

Serve on a bed of hot, fluffy rice.

¼ cup	vegetable oil
½ cup	onion, chopped
3 tablespoons	unsweetened coconut,* chopped
4 teaspoons	curry powder
2 – 3 cloves	garlic, minced
2 pounds	assorted raw vegetables (potatoes, cauliflower, broccoli, carrots, zucchini, etc.), cut into bite-size pieces
3 cups	tomatoes, peeled and diced
2 cups	water
2 teaspoons	salt
4 teaspoons	sugar
dash	thyme

Heat oil in large skillet with cover. Add onion, coconut, curry powder and garlic. Cook, stirring occasionally, until onion is tender. Add vegetables, tomato, water, salt, sugar and thyme. Cover tightly and cook over low heat until vegetables are tender, approximately 45 minutes.

Brussels Sprouts
Au Gratin

Serves 6

20 ounces	**fresh Brussels sprouts, blanched**
	freshly ground pepper to taste
4 strips	**bacon, cut into ½-inch pieces**
¾ cup	**whipping cream**
½ cup	**bread crumbs**
	butter
½ teaspoon	**paprika**

Preheat oven to 400 degrees. Place Brussels sprouts in baking dish and sprinkle with pepper. Fry bacon until cooked but not crispy. Add to baking dish. Pour in cream and top with bread crumbs. Dot with butter and sprinkle on paprika. Bake uncovered for 25 to 30 minutes.

Cut a shallow X in the stem ends of raw Brussels sprouts to allow the stems and leaves to cook evenly.

Curried Zucchini

Serves 10

2 teaspoons	butter or margarine
2 cups	zucchini, chopped
1 cup	onion, chopped
½ cup	yellow bell pepper, seeded and chopped
1½ cups	plum tomatoes, seeded and chopped
1 teaspoon	brown sugar
¾ teaspoon	curry powder
	salt and freshly ground pepper to taste
2 tablespoons	Parmesan cheese,* grated

Melt butter over low heat in a large skillet. Add zucchini, onion and pepper and sauté just until tender. Add tomatoes, brown sugar, curry powder, salt and pepper. Mix thoroughly. Cover and cook for two minutes. Sprinkle with Parmesan cheese and serve.

Herbed Potatoes

Serves 6

2¼ pounds	potatoes, peeled and cubed
5 tablespoons	olive oil*
7 tablespoons	butter
10	sage leaves, chopped
2	fresh rosemary sprigs, chopped
1	parsley sprig, chopped
1 clove	garlic, pressed
	salt and freshly ground pepper to taste

Preheat oven to 450 degrees. Heat olive oil and butter in a large, ovenproof skillet. Add potatoes and cook until golden brown. Put the skillet into the oven for about 20 minutes to finish cooking the potatoes. Combine sage, rosemary, parsley, garlic, salt and pepper and sprinkle over potatoes. Toss to distribute seasonings evenly and serve.

A holiday party means gather the best mix of food and good company. But don't be surprised if your Korean auntie brings the Japanese sushi or the Chinese noodles.

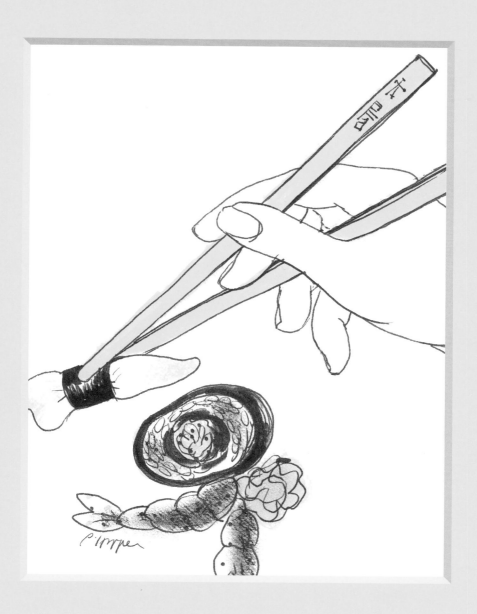

Eggs, Cheese, Rice and Pasta

Hanauma Bay Pasta

Serves 8

4 tablespoons	olive oil*
3 cups	fresh basil
2 tablespoons	fresh lemon juice
¼ cup	extra virgin olive oil*
	salt and freshly ground pepper to taste
1½ pounds	large shrimp, shelled and deveined
2 cloves	garlic, crushed
½ pound	bow-tie pasta
2 cups	frozen peas, thawed and drained
2	tomatoes, seeded and cut into ¼-inch cubes
Garnish:	*Fresh basil and diced tomatoes*

Place basil in a food processor with 1 tablespoon olive oil and process until smooth. Remove to a bowl and add lemon juice, extra virgin olive oil, salt, pepper and garlic. Set aside. In a saucepan, sauté shrimp and garlic in remaining oil until shrimp are opaque, about 2 to 4 minutes. In a pot of boiling salted water, cook pasta until al dente. Drain and combine with shrimp in a large bowl. Toss with basil puree, peas and tomatoes. Adjust seasonings and garnish with slivered basil leaves and diced tomatoes.

Wild Rice Casserole

Serves 12

4	green onions, chopped, white part only
2 – 3 cloves	garlic, minced
1 pound	fresh mushrooms, sliced
½ pound	butter
2 cups	wild rice
½ teaspoon	thyme
¼ teaspoon	tumeric
	salt and freshly ground pepper
1½ cups	pecans, chopped
5 cups	chicken or beef broth

Preheat oven to 350 degrees. Sauté onions, garlic and mushrooms in butter until tender. Stir in rice, seasonings and pecans and mix well. Turn into a 2-quart casserole and pour broth over rice. Cover and bake until broth is absorbed, about 1½ hours.

Note: The rice may be prepared ahead and refrigerated. To serve, return casserole to room temperature before baking.

Spinach Pasta with Gorgonzola Sauce

Serves 4 – 6

¼ pound	**Gorgonzola cheese,* crumbled**
⅓ cup	**milk**
3 tablespoons	**butter**
⅓ cup	**heavy cream**
1 clove	**garlic, minced**
1 pound	**spinach fettucine or spaghetti**
⅓ cup	**fresh Parmesan cheese,* grated**
3 tablespoons	**parsley, chopped**
Garnish:	*Grated Parmesan cheese**

In a large skillet, combine the Gorgonzola cheese, milk and butter. Cook over low heat, stirring until cheese is melted and sauce is smooth. Add cream and garlic and stir until the sauce is hot and well blended. Cook pasta in a pot of boiling salted water. Drain and transfer to serving bowl. Add the cheese sauce, Parmesan cheese and parsley and toss lightly until coated. Garnish and serve immediately.

Szechuan Noodle Toss

Serves 8

2 tablespoons	sesame oil,* divided
4	green onions, cut into 1-inch pieces
1 carrot	sliced
1	red bell pepper, julienned
1	green bell pepper, julienned
1 (15-ounce) can	baby corn,* drained
1 (8-ounce) can	water chestnuts,* drained and sliced
8 ounces	garden spirals or small pasta shells, cooked
¼ cup	soy sauce*
2 tablespoons	rice vinegar*
½ teaspoon	crushed red pepper
1 teaspoon	fresh ginger,* minced

Sauté green onions in 1 tablespoon sesame oil until
tender, about 1 minute. Add carrot and cook approximately
1 minute. Add peppers and cook another minute. Add corn and
water chestnuts and cook until vegetables are tender. Combine
cooked vegetables with pasta. Mix remaining oil, soy sauce,
vinegar, red pepper and ginger and pour over pasta and
vegetables. Toss and serve. This may be served warm or
at room temperature.

Garden Harvest Pasta

Serves 6 – 8

4	medium tomatoes, peeled, seeded and coarsely chopped
4 cloves	garlic, minced
½ cup	fresh basil, chopped
1 tablespoon	fresh mint, chopped
1 teaspoon	salt
½ teaspoon	freshly ground pepper
¼ teaspoon	hot pepper flakes
½ cup	olive oil*
1 pound	small pasta shells
½ cup	Parmesan cheese,* grated
¼ pound	Fontina cheese,* grated
½ cup	broccoli, chopped
½ cup	cauliflower, chopped
½ cup	green bell pepper, chopped
½ cup	red onion, chopped
¼ cup	red bell pepper, chopped

Combine tomatoes, garlic, basil, mint, salt, pepper, hot pepper flakes and olive oil. Let stand at room temperature for 2 – 3 hours, tossing occasionally. Cook pasta for 8 – 10 minutes. Drain and transfer to a large bowl. Spoon off ¼ cup liquid from tomatoes and toss with pasta to coat. While pasta is still warm, add Parmesan and Fontina cheeses and toss until cheeses begin to melt. Add tomato mixture and toss until mixed. Serve warm or at room temperature.

Linguine with Two Cheeses

Serves 6

¼ cup	butter
¾ cup	heavy cream
½ cup	Cheddar cheese, grated
½ cup	Parmesan cheese,* grated
	salt to taste
1 pound	linguine, cooked and drained
Garnish:	*Grated Parmesan cheese* and*
	1 teaspoon chopped parsley

Melt butter in a small saucepan. Add cream, cheeses and salt, stirring frequently until the cheeses melt and form a smooth sauce. Pour sauce over pasta. Garnish and serve immediately.

Sweet Curry Pilaf

Serves 6 – 8

Serve with lamb.

4 tablespoons	vegetable oil
½ teaspoon	curry powder
½ teaspoon	tumeric
2 cups	long grain rice
4 cups	chicken broth
1½ tablespoons	soy sauce*
½ cup	golden raisins

In saucepan, combine oil, curry, tumeric and rice. Cook over low heat for 5 minutes, stirring occasionally. Add chicken broth, soy sauce and raisins and heat to boiling. Stir, cover and simmer over low heat until liquid is absorbed, about 15 to 20 minutes.

Mushroom Potato Frittata *Serves 6*

10	**eggs**
2 teaspoons	**Tabasco**
1 cup	**mushrooms, chopped**
1 cup	**Cheddar cheese, grated**
1 cup	**green onion, chopped**
1 cup	**potatoes, parboiled, drained and diced**
⅓ cup	**olive oil***
1 teaspoon	**dill**
½ teaspoon	**salt**
	freshly ground pepper to taste
Garnish:	*Chopped parsley*

Preheat oven to 450 degrees. Beat eggs and Tabasco until frothy. Add mushrooms and cheese. In a 10-inch oven-proof skillet, saute the onion and potato in olive oil for 10 minutes. Pour egg mixture over onions and potatoes. Sprinkle with dill, salt and pepper. Bake in lower third of oven for 15 to 20 minutes, or until frittata has puffed and is firm when pan is shaken. Allow to cool slightly before cutting. Garnish with chopped parsley.

Colorful Pasta Salad

Serves 12

¼ pound	Provolone cheese, cubed
¼ pound	hard salami, cubed
¼ pound	pepperoni, cubed
1	medium onion, diced
1	medium green bell pepper, diced
3 stalks	celery, diced
6	fresh tomatoes, diced
1 (2¼-ounce) can	sliced black olives, drained
1 (7-ounce) jar	green olives, drained and sliced
1 pound	small tricolor pasta, cooked

Dressing

1¼ cups	vegetable oil
⅔ cup	cider vinegar
1 tablespoon	salt
1 tablespoon	oregano
1 teaspoon	coarsely ground black pepper

Mix dressing ingredients in a bowl. Pour over salad and toss until well combined. Cover and chill for 4 to 6 hours.

Chili Cheese Souffle

Serves 8

A spicy quiche without the crust.

10	eggs
½ cup	flour
1 teaspoon	baking powder
½ teaspoon	salt
1 pint	small curd cottage cheese
1 pound	Monterey Jack cheese, grated
½ cup	butter, melted
2 (4-ounce) cans	green chilies, diced
2	jalapeno peppers, diced

Preheat oven to 350 degrees. Beat eggs until lemon colored. Stir in flour, baking powder and salt. Add cheeses and butter. Blend until smooth. Stir in chilies. Pour into a greased 9 x 13-inch pan. Bake for 35 minutes or until top is slightly browned and inside is set.

Julie's Rotini
With Artichokes

Serves 6

This tangy dish tastes great either hot or cold with a squeeze of lemon.

2 tablespoons	olive oil*
2 cloves	garlic, minced
1(14½-ounce) can	stewed tomatoes, drained and chopped
½ cup	black olives, sliced
¾ cup	marinated artichoke hearts, sliced
1½ cups	vegetable rotini (garden spirals), cooked
	salt and freshly ground pepper to taste
Garnish:	*Grated fresh Romano cheese**

In a large saucepan, sauté garlic in oil. Add tomatoes, black olives and artichokes and cook over low heat for 10 to 20 minutes. Add pasta and stir until heated through. Add salt and pepper. Top with Romano cheese and serve.

Sausage and Spinach Bake

Serves 6 – 8

1 pound	**pork sausage**
2 (10-ounce) packages	**frozen chopped spinach, thawed, cooked and drained**
½ teaspoon	**salt**
½ teaspoon	**freshly ground pepper**
1 dozen	**eggs, beaten**

Sauté sausage until well done. Drain excess grease. Reduce heat and add spinach, salt and pepper. Add eggs. Cook, stirring constantly, until eggs are set. Serve immediately with warm bread or biscuits.

Spaghetti Michi

Serves 4 – 6

A chunky vegetarian spaghetti sauce.

2 tablespoons	olive oil*
2 cloves	garlic, pressed
1 medium	onion, coarsely chopped
1 (28-ounce) can	whole tomatoes, including juice, coarsely chopped
½ cup	red wine
1 pint	fresh mushrooms, halved
1 large	red bell pepper, halved and sliced
1 large	yellow bell pepper, halved and sliced
2 teaspoons	oregano
1 teaspoon	basil
1 teaspoon	thyme
	salt and freshly ground pepper to taste
1 pound	spaghetti, cooked and drained

Sauté onion and garlic in olive oil until limp. Add tomatoes, wine, mushrooms, peppers and spices. Simmer until peppers are limp. Serve over spaghetti in a bowl.

Variation: Add 2 pounds of Italian sausage for a non-vegetarian sauce.

Shrimp with Vegetables and Pasta

Serves 6 – 8

Serve in shallow bowls with crusty French bread to soak up the sauce.

1½ cups	chicken broth
½ cup	white wine
2 cloves	garlic, crushed
5 ounces	cavatelli or other small, shaped pasta
2 cups	stewed tomatoes, drained and coarsely chopped
	salt and freshly ground pepper to taste
¾ cup	butter
1½ cups	onions, chopped
1 cup	scallions, chopped
½ pound	mushrooms, sliced
2½ pounds	jumbo white shrimp or tiger prawns, cooked, shelled and deveined
¾ cup	butter, melted
½ cup	Parmesan cheese,* grated

Bring chicken broth, wine and garlic to a boil in a saucepan. Add pasta and cook until al dente, stirring occasionally. Add tomatoes, salt and pepper. Simmer for 5 minutes. Meanwhile, melt ¾ cup butter in a skillet. Sauté onions, scallions and mushrooms until tender, about 6 minutes. Add vegetables to pasta and tomato sauce. Stir in shrimp and melted butter and heat through. Adjust seasonings. Stir in grated Parmesan cheese and serve.

Paniolo Spanish Rice

Good served with cole slaw.

¼ cup	water
1 cup	onion, chopped
¾ cup	green bell pepper, chopped
1 cup	uncooked rice
3½ cups	stewed tomatoes, drained and coarsely chopped
1 teaspoon	salt
½ teaspoon	freshly ground pepper
1 small	bay leaf
1 teaspoon	cumin
1 (4-ounce) can	mild chili peppers, diced
½ cup	Cheddar cheese, shredded

Preheat oven to 350 degrees. Combine all ingredients except cheese and pour into a 2-quart casserole. Cover and bake for 1 hour and 15 minutes, stirring occasionally. During the last ten minutes of baking time, remove cover and sprinkle with cheese.

*Some ancient Hawaiian warriors
wore dignified masks made from gourds.
The mask symbol has made a comeback
in the wake of renewed cultural awareness.*

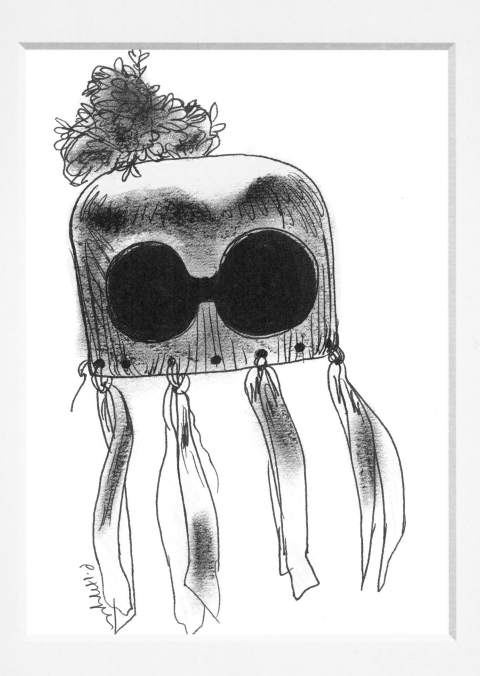

Sauces, Condiments and Da Kine

243

Curried Fruit Compote

Makes 2 – 3 quarts

This is delicious with baked ham.

1 (16-ounce) can	pear slices, drained, reserve syrup
1 (16-ounce) can	apricot slices, drained
1 (16-ounce) can	pineapple* chunks, drained
1 (4-ounce) jar	maraschino cherries, drained
1 large	ripe papaya,* peeled, seeded, halved and sliced (optional)
3 large	firm, ripe bananas, sliced (optional)
2 tablespoons	butter, melted
2 tablespoons	pear syrup, from pear slices
2 tablespoons	dark brown sugar
1 tablespoon	curry powder
2 teaspoons	cornstarch
½ teaspoon	lemon peel, grated

Place fruit in a glass baking dish. Mix 2 tablespoons pear syrup, butter, brown sugar, curry powder, cornstarch, and lemon peel and pour over the fruit. Let stand for several hours to draw out the juices and enhance flavor. About 45 minutes prior to serving, preheat oven to 325 degrees. Carefully stir fruit and bake uncovered for 30 minutes. Stir occasionally during baking.

Haole Plum Sauce

Makes 2 cups

Use as a glaze on chicken, ham or Cornish game hens.

1½ cups	red plum jam
1½ tablespoons	prepared mustard
1½ tablespoons	horseradish
1½ teaspoons	lemon juice

Combine ingredients in a small saucepan and cook over low heat until warmed through, stirring constantly.

Note: This keeps indefinitely in the refrigerator.

Pineapple Salsa

Makes 2 cups

½	fresh pineapple,* cut into ¼-inch cubes
2	tomatoes, seeded, cut into ¼-inch cubes
½	medium Maui onion,* cut into ¼-inch cubes
¼ cup	Chinese parsley,* chopped
½	teaspoon garlic, minced
1	jalapeno pepper, seeded and minced
1	teaspoon coriander seed, crushed
¾	teaspoon cumin
½	teaspoon salt

Mix all ingredients together. Cover and chill for at least one hour. Serve with grilled chicken or fish.

Papaya Salsa

Makes 1 quart

This salsa is a refreshing complement to the smoky, salty flavor of grilled seafood.

3 cups	ripe papaya,* diced
1 cup	tomato, diced
1 cup	red bell pepper, finely diced
1½ cups	red onion, diced
½	jalapeno pepper, seeded and finely chopped
2 teaspoons	ground cumin
2 tablespoons	extra-virgin olive oil*
2½ tablespoons	red wine vinegar*
6 tablespoons	freshly squeezed lime juice
2 tablespoons	freshly squeezed lemon juice
1 teaspoon	freshly ground black pepper
dash	Tabasco
1 cup	Chinese parsley,* loosely packed and coarsely chopped

Combine all ingredients in a large porcelain or glass bowl. Toss thoroughly. Cover and let stand for 1 or 2 hours. Serve chilled or at room temperature.

Note: Salsa will keep in the refrigerator for up to a week.

When Captain Cook anchored his ship in Kealakekua Bay on the Big Island in 1778, he is said to have brought seeds of the papaya with him from Central America. They were planted, spread throughout Hawai'i, and became the fruit of the chiefs or ali'i. Several varieties are known locally: Solo, Puna and Sunrise, with flesh colors ranging from light yellow to deep salmon.

Satay Sauce

Makes 1½ cups

A peanut dipping sauce for chicken, vegetables or apples.

¾ cup	chicken stock
1 cup	regular or crunchy peanut butter
¼ cup	ketjap manis*
¼ cup	shallots or green onions, including some tops, chopped
3 cloves	garlic, minced
1½ tablespoons	brown sugar
2 tablespoons	fresh lemon or lime juice
1 teaspoon	chili pepper flakes
¼ teaspoon	fresh ginger,* grated

In a saucepan, bring chicken stock to a boil. Add remaining ingredients and stir until smooth. Let cool to room temperature before serving.

Note: Sauce may be prepared up to 3 hours ahead. Cover and refrigerate. Bring sauce to room temperature before serving.

Sweet and Sour Sauce for Fish

Makes 1 cup

¼ cup	sugar
2 teaspoons	cornstarch
	dash salt
3 tablespoons	cold water
2 tablespoons	white vinegar
1 tablespoon	soy sauce*
1 tablespoon	dry white wine

Combine ingredients in a saucepan and cook over low heat until bubbly and thick, stirring frequently. Serve warm as a dipping sauce or use to baste fish before grilling.

Aunty Olive's Barbecue Sauce

Makes 3 cups

Great for grilling, broiling, or barbecue.

1 cup	catsup
1/3 cup	oyster sauce*
1 cup	brown sugar
3/4 cup	soy sauce*
1	onion, minced

Combine ingredients and mix well. Marinate ribs or chicken for at least 1/2 hour but preferably overnight.

Zesty Cranberry Sauce

Makes 1 cup

1 (10-ounce) package	fresh or frozen cranberries
3/4 cup	water
1 1/2 cups	sugar
4 1/2 tablespoons	orange marmalade
	juice of 1 lemon
	juice of 1 lime

Rinse and drain cranberries. Boil water and sugar for 5 minutes. Add cranberries and cook without stirring until skins pop and cranberries are transparent, approximately 8 minutes. Remove from heat and stir in marmalade. Add lemon juice and lime juice and stir. Pour into serving dish. Cover and refrigerate.

Tangy Cucumber Sauce

Makes 2½ cups

Great with barbecued salmon.

1 large	cucumber, peeled, seeded and thinly sliced
	salt
1 cup	mayonnaise
1 cup	sour cream
1 (4-ounce) jar	creamy horseradish
⅛ teaspoon	salt
⅛ teaspoon	white pepper
1 tablespoon	tarragon vinegar*

Place cucumber slices on paper towels and lightly sprinkle with salt. Let stand for 10 minutes and squeeze out the liquid. Combine mayonnaise, sour cream and horseradish. Stir in salt, white pepper and vinegar. Toss cucumbers with sauce. Note: Sauce will keep in the refrigerator for 10 days.

Variation: To make Cucumber Dill Sauce, substitute 2 tablespoons fresh dill or 1½ teaspoons dried dill for horseradish and 1 tablespoon lemon juice for vinegar.

Sance's Mustard Sauce

Makes 2 cups

Great with ham.

⅔ cup	dry mustard
⅔ cup	vinegar
⅔ cup	brown sugar
2	eggs, well beaten
⅓ cup	honey

In a medium saucepan, mix mustard and vinegar together until smooth. Add brown sugar and beaten eggs. Cook over medium heat until smooth and very thick, stirring constantly. Remove from heat and add honey. Serve at room temperature or chilled as a dipping sauce for ham or other appetizers. Sauce may be stored in the refrigerator for several weeks.

Papaya Curry Marinade

Makes 1 cup

Use as a marinade for poultry or pork.

1	ripe papaya,* peeled and seeded
½ cup	orange juice
¼ cup	vegetable oil
2 tablespoons	lemon juice
1½ teaspoons	curry powder
2 teaspoons	salt

Place ingredients in a blender or food processor and blend well. Spoon over meat and marinate overnight.

Cranberry Chutney

Makes 2 cups

½ cup	onion, sliced
6 tablespoons	brown sugar
¼ cup	sugar
½ cup	water
6 tablespoons	cider vinegar
1	Granny Smith apple, peeled, seeded and diced
¼ teaspoon	salt
½ teaspoon	fresh ginger,* grated
¼ teaspoon	mace
¼ teaspoon	curry powder
	grated zest of 1 orange
1 quart	cranberries, washed and drained
¼ cup	currants
	strained juice of 1 orange

Simmer onion, sugars and water for 30 minutes. Bring to a boil and stir in vinegar, apples, seasonings and orange zest. Boil slowly for 30 minutes. Add cranberries, currants and orange juice and boil until cranberries burst, about 10 minutes. Remove from heat and let cool. Cover and refrigerate until serving.

A relative of the cranberry, the ohelo shrub is indigenous to Hawai'i, growing mostly in East Maui and on the island of Hawai'i. It grows wild in high elevations on lava flows and volcanic ash. The delicate thornless bushes produce small red or yellow berries that may be eaten raw or cooked in pies, sauces and jams. Because the plant grows well on Kilauea crater on the Big Island of Hawai'i, it is considered sacred to the volcano goddess Pele. It was customary for Hawaiians to offer some fruit to her before eating any themselves.

The warm, orange glow of an ilima lei,
so carefully sewn with paper-thin blossoms.
No wonder it was a lei of Hawaiian royalty.

Desserts

Desserts

Hot Fudge
Sundae Crepes

Makes 12 crepes

Elegant and impressive for small parties.

Batter

6 tablespoons	flour
6 tablespoons	cocoa
¼ teaspoon	salt
2	eggs
2	egg yolks
1 tablespoon	sugar
¼ cup	vegetable oil
⅓ cup	milk

Filling

1 quart	vanilla frozen yogurt or ice cream
	chocolate sauce

Combine batter ingredients in a blender or food processor and blend until smooth. Chill batter 1 to 2 hours. Heat a 6 or 7-inch crepe pan until a drop of water sizzles and jumps about the pan. Coat pan with butter. Pour about 2 tablespoons batter into pan and tilt to spread evenly. Cook until surface looks dry, approximately 45 to 60 seconds. Run knife around edge of crepe to loosen and invert pan to let crepe drop out. Fill unbrowned side with scoops of frozen yogurt or ice cream and fold. Top with chocolate sauce and serve.

Papaya Sorbet

Serves 8 – 10

3 large	**papayas,* peeled, seeded and pureed (about 2½ cups)**
¼ cup	**lemon juice**
1 envelope	**unflavored gelatin**
½ cup	**orange juice**
¾ cup	**sugar**
¼ cup	**honey**
1 cup	**whipping cream**

Combine papaya puree and lemon juice. Soften gelatin in orange juice, then dissolve over boiling water. Blend sugar and honey with whipping cream. Gradually stir in gelatin and papaya puree. Pour into ice trays and freeze for 1 hour or until half frozen. Beat the mixture, then return to freezer and freeze completely.

Goody Goody

Serves 8 – 10

A Maui favorite on hot sunny days.

3 (12-ounce) cans	**strawberry soda**
1 (14-ounce) can	**sweetened condensed milk**

Mix strawberry soda and sweetened condensed milk and pour into a metal baking dish. Freeze until partially frozen, about 1 to 2 hours. Beat the mixture, then return to freezer and freeze completely.

This cool, sherbet-like treat, originally named Guri Guri,* is sold at Maui Mall and at a stand near the old stadium park here in Honolulu.

Almond Caramel Meringue   *Serves 6*

Meringue

2¼ cups	sugar, divided
6	egg whites
pinch	cream of tartar
½ teaspoon	vanilla

Preheat oven to 275 degrees. Heat 1¼ cups sugar in a saucepan over low heat, stirring constantly, until sugar is melted and golden brown. Pour syrup into a 9½-inch ring mold and tilt the mold until its sides are well coated. (Do not scrape or wash saucepan, as it will be used it to make the sauce.) Beat egg whites and cream of tartar until foamy. Beat in ½ cup sugar, a tablespoon at a time. Continue beating until the whites are very stiff. Beat in vanilla. Fold in remaining ½ cup sugar. Spoon mixture into the caramel coated mold, carefully smoothing out any air pockets. Place mold, uncovered, in a larger pan containing ½-inch warm water. Bake one hour or until the meringue is high, firm, and light brown on top. Quickly loosen the edges of the meringue with a knife dipped in cold water to prevent tearing. Immediately unmold, allowing the caramel liquid to drip over the meringue.

Sauce

1 cup	milk
½ cup	heavy cream
6	egg yolks
1 teaspoon	almond extract

continued...

Warm milk in the same pan in which the sugar caramelized. Beat the cream and egg yolks together. Add to the warm milk and stir briskly with a flat whisk over low to moderate heat until sauce is as thick as very heavy cream. Do not allow to boil. Immediately remove from heat. Add almond extract. Refrigerate until serving time, then serve from a separate bowl.

Chocolate Mousse   *Serves 4*

1 envelope	**unflavored gelatin**
¼ cup	**water**
4 ounces	**semi-sweet chocolate**
2 ounces	**unsweetened chocolate**
1¼ cups	**heavy whipping cream**
¼ cup	**sugar**
Garnish:	*Chocolate shavings*

In a small saucepan, sprinkle gelatin over water and let soften for 3 minutes. Cook over low heat until gelatin dissolves. Bring mixture to a simmer and add sugar, stirring until dissolved. Do not boil. Set aside. Melt chocolate in a double boiler. Transfer the melted chocolate to a separate bowl. Gradually add gelatin mixture to chocolate, whisking with each addition. Whip cream and sugar into soft peaks. Set aside enough to garnish top of mousse. Stir half of the whipped cream into chocolate mixture to lighten. Then take chocolate mixture and, while electric mixer is on low, pour into remaining whipped cream. Blend on low to incorporate chocolate. Increase speed to high and whip for a total of 10 to 15 seconds. Spoon into parfait or champagne glasses and chill for 1 to 2 hours or until firm. Garnish with reserved whipped cream and chocolate shavings.

To make chocolate shavings, run a vegetable peeler down the side of a slightly warmed chocolate bar.

Grandmother's Chocolate Sauce

Makes 2 cups

5 ounces	**unsweetened chocolate**
8 tablespoons	**butter**
1 cup	**cream**
2 cups	**sugar**

Melt chocolate and butter over low heat in a heavy saucepan. Add cream and sugar. Cook slowly over low heat, stirring frequently. Cook until sauce starts to thicken, about 10 minutes. Serve over coconut, peppermint, coffee, or vanilla ice cream. Store sauce in the refrigerator for up to 1 week.

Onolicious Chocolate Sauce

Makes 2 cups

This heavenly sauce makes an excellent gift at Christmas time.

3 tablespoons	**butter**
4 ounces	**unsweetened chocolate**
⅔ cup	**evaporated milk**
2 cups	**powdered sugar**
1 teaspoon	**vanilla**

Melt butter and chocolate over low heat in a heavy saucepan. Add milk and stir until blended. Add sugar and beat until smooth. Stir in vanilla. Serve over ice cream, fruit or angel food cake.

Note: Sauce keeps well in the refrigerator.

Crunchy Baked Mangoes   *Serves 4 – 6*

Island version of apple crisp.

4 medium	**mangoes,* peeled and thinly sliced**
½ cup	**sugar**
¾ cup	**quick-cooking rolled oats**
¾ cup	**brown sugar**
½ cup	**flour**
1 teaspoon	**cinnamon**
½ cup	**butter or margarine**

Preheat oven to 350 degrees. Toss mangoes with sugar. Place in a greased 8-inch round pan. Combine oats, brown sugar, flour and cinnamon. Cut in butter until mixture is crumbly. Sprinkle evenly over mangoes. Bake for 35 to 40 minutes or until top crust is browned and crisp. Serve warm with ice cream.

Note: Ripeness of mangoes will determine the amount of sugar needed. Use less sugar with riper mangoes.

Undoubtedly the most popular fruit tree in the state, the first mango trees were introduced to Hawai'i from Manila in 1824 by Captain John Meek of the Kamehameha. Indigenous to Southern Asia, the mango has made its way to many subtropical regions of the world. It is a medium-sized fruit, with patches of crimson, purple, green and golden yellow when ripe. The most common of mangoes, Hayden, comes from Florida, while the Pirie has its origins in India. There are many varieties of mangoes, but the better ones are chosen for their sweet flavor, smooth texture and juiciness. It is an excellent source of vitamin A, and when half ripe or green, a good source of vitamin C. Mango season runs throughout the summer. It is eaten fresh as a dessert fruit, used for sauces, in salads or in desserts. Green, it can be made into chutney, pickled or dried and preserved as mango seed.

Apple Sweetbread Pudding

Serves 8 – 10

2 cups	apples, peeled and thinly sliced
3 tablespoons *plus*	
½ cup	butter, divided
2 tablespoons	lemon juice
½ cup	brown sugar
2 tablespoons *plus*	
1 teaspoon	cinnamon, divided
1 (1-pound) loaf	sweetbread
1 cup	raisins
2 cups	milk, scalded
1 cup	sugar
5	eggs
1 teaspoon	vanilla

Preheat oven to 350 degrees. Grease a 9 x 13-inch pan. Tear bread into 2-inch pieces and place in pan. In a medium saucepan, sauté apples in 3 tablespoons butter and lemon juice over medium-low heat. Add brown sugar and 2 tablespoons cinnamon and cook until sauce thickens. Remove from heat and set aside. Spread apple mixture over bread pieces. Sprinkle with raisins. Combine milk and ½ cup butter and stir until melted. Stir in sugar. Beat eggs and vanilla in a separate bowl. Add eggs and remaining 1 teaspoon cinnamon to milk mixture and mix well. Pour over bread. Bake for 30 minutes. Serve warm or chilled.

Fruit with Amaretto Sauce

Serves 4 – 6

3 cups	fresh raspberries, strawberries or peaches, sliced
3 tablespoons	amaretto liqueur or macadamia nut liqueur
3 tablespoons	sugar

Toss fruit with liqueur and sugar. Set aside and chill.

Amaretto Sauce

8 ounces	ricotta cheese, softened
8 ounces	cream cheese, softened
½ cup	sugar
4	egg yolks
2 tablespoons	cream
3 tablespoons	amaretto liqueur
Garnish:	*Mint sprigs*

In a food processor, combine sauce ingredients and process until smooth. Chill. For each serving, place fruit into dessert bowl. Spoon sauce over fruit and garnish with mint.

Kascaran

A crunchy, chewy Filipino sweet.

1 pound	**mochiko* flour**
1 (7-ounce) package	**sweetened coconut***
2 cups	**water**
½ cup	**sugar**
¾ teaspoon	**baking powder**
	vegetable oil for deep frying
¼ cup	**honey or sugar**

Mix mochiko flour, coconut, water, sugar and baking powder. Pinch off heaping teaspoons of dough and form into ovals. Heat the oil to 375 degrees in a deep-fat fryer or heavy kettle. Fry the cookies in batches until golden brown, turning once, about 10 to 15 minutes. When first dropped into oil, cookies will sink to the bottom and stay. Loosen from bottom after 5 minutes of cooking so they float. Remove from oil and drain on paper towels. While cookies are still warm, coat with honey or sugar. Cool on wire racks.

Almond Float

The traditional ending to a Chinese banquet.

3 envelopes	**unflavored gelatin**
3½ cups	**water, divided**
1 cup	**sugar**
1 cup	**evaporated milk**
2 tablespoons	**almond extract**
3 (11-ounce) cans	**mandarin oranges**
1 bunch	**fresh mint**

Dissolve gelatin in ½ cup cold water. In a medium pan, combine sugar, evaporated milk and 3 cups of water. Cook over low heat, stirring constantly, until mixture comes to a boil. Add gelatin to pan and cook for 2 more minutes. Cool slightly and add almond extract. Pour into a 9-inch square glass dish or into individual serving dishes and refrigerate for several hours. To serve, cut float into cubes, top with mandarin oranges and garnish with fresh mint.

Fluffy Almond Puff

Serves 10 – 12

Great for special breakfasts or dinner parties.

1 cup	butter, divided
2 cups	unsifted flour
¼ teaspoon	salt
2 tablespoons	cold water
1 cup	water
3	eggs
1 teaspoon	almond extract

Preheat oven to 425 degrees. With a pastry blender, cut ½ cup butter into 1 cup flour and salt until mixture resembles coarse meal. Add cold water and mix well to form soft dough. Divide in half. On large baking sheet, press each half into a strip 3 inches wide and 12 inches long. Set aside. In a medium saucepan, bring remaining ½ cup butter and water to boil. Remove from heat. Immediately stir in remaining 1 cup flour. Beat until smooth. Add eggs, one at a time, beating well after each addition. Beat in almond extract. Spread evenly over pastry. Bake until dark golden brown, about 30 minutes. Frost with powdered sugar icing. Slice thinly on the diagonal and serve.

Powdered Sugar Icing

2 cups	powdered sugar
1 tablespoon	butter, softened
3 – 4 tablespoons	milk
⅛ teaspoon	salt
1 teaspoon	vanilla

Mix sugar with butter, milk, salt and vanilla. Stir in 3 to 4 tablespoons milk, a teaspoon at a time, until frosting is of desired consistency. Spoon over tops of pastry and drizzle down sides.

Baked *Mochi*

3 cups	coconut milk*
2¼ cups	brown sugar
1½ cups	water
5 cups	mochiko* flour
1½ teaspoons	baking soda
1 (18-ounce) can	koshian*
	katakuri-ko*

Preheat oven to 350 degrees. Mix coconut milk, brown sugar, water, mochiko flour, baking soda and koshian in a large bowl. Pour into greased 9 x 13-inch pan. Bake for one hour. Cool overnight. Cut into 1-inch by 1½-inch slices. (Use a plastic knife to prevent sticking.) Coat each strip of mochi in katakuri-ko and serve. Store in an airtight container.

Mochi may be colored for special occasions. Chichi mochi (chichi means milk), a pink or white mochi with a small amount of milk added, is served on Girls' Day. Ceremonial dolls are the traditional gifts on this day. On Boys' Day, families fly wind socks shaped like koi, or carp, for each boy in the house. The carp symbolizes courage, fortitude, ambition and perseverence. Mochi eaten on this day is wrapped in either a fig or mulberry leaf.

Frozen Cranberry Soufflé

Makes 5 cups

½ cup	whipping cream
¼ cup *plus* 1 tablespoon	sugar, divided
1 teaspoon	vanilla
1 (16-ounce) can	cranberry sauce, pureed
3 large	bananas, pureed
1 (15¼-ounce) can	crushed pineapple,* drained
2 teaspoons	lemon juice
½ cup	pecans, chopped
1 cup	sour cream

Beat whipping cream, 1 tablespoon sugar and vanilla until stiff. Set aside. Combine ¼ cup sugar, cranberry puree, banana puree, pineapple, lemon juice, pecans and sour cream and blend together. Fold whipped cream into fruit mixture. Pour into ice cream canister and freeze according to manufacturer's instructions.

Chill the mixing bowl and beaters to obtain maximum volume for whipped cream.

Luscious Lemon Sauce   *Makes 1½ cups*

2	**eggs**
1 cup *plus*	
1 tablespoon	**sugar, divided**
⅓ cup	**frozen lemon juice concentrate, thawed**
1 tablespoon	**cornstarch**
½ cup	**water**
2 teaspoons	**vanilla, divided**
½ cup	**whipping cream**
	assorted fresh fruit cut in bite-size pieces – pineapple,* strawberries, grapes, watermelon, etc.

Beat eggs until foamy. Gradually beat in ½ cup sugar and lemon juice. Set aside. In a saucepan, combine ½ cup sugar, cornstarch, and water. Cook over low heat, stirring until thickened. Remove from heat. Gradually beat in egg mixture. Cook over low heat, stirring constantly until thickened. Stir in 1 teaspoon vanilla. Refrigerate for 2 hours. Beat whipping cream, 1 tablespoon sugar and 1 teaspoon vanilla until stiff. Fold whipped cream into lemon sauce and spoon into serving bowl. Serve as a dipping sauce for fresh fruit.

Vanilla Cake

1 (12-ounce) box	**vanilla wafers**
1 cup	**butter**
2 cups	**sugar**
6	**eggs**
½ cup	**milk**
1 cup	**walnuts, chopped**
1 (7-ounce) package	**flaked coconut***
	powdered sugar

Preheat oven to 325 degrees. Grease and flour a 10-inch tube pan. Crush or grind vanilla wafers and set aside. Cream butter and sugar until light and fluffy. Add eggs, one at a time, beating well after each addition. Add wafers and milk. Fold in nuts and coconut. Bake for 1 hour and 15 minutes. Dust top with powdered sugar before serving.

Apple Spice Cake

Just like Grandma used to make.

½ cup	brown sugar
1 cup	sugar
½ cup	shortening
2	eggs
1 cup	buttermilk
1 teaspoon	baking soda
½ teaspoon	salt
1½ teaspoons	cinnamon
2½ cups	flour
1 teaspoon	vanilla
3 cups	apples, peeled and diced

Preheat oven to 350 degrees. Grease and flour a
9 x 13-inch baking pan. Cream sugars and shortening. Add eggs,
buttermilk, baking soda, salt, cinnamon, flour and vanilla and mix
well. Fold in apples. Pour into prepared pan. Sprinkle topping
over batter and bake for 50 to 55 minutes.

Topping

⅓ cup	brown sugar
⅓ cup	sugar
1 teaspoon	cinnamon
½ cup	walnuts, chopped

Combine brown sugar, sugar and cinnamon and blend
well. Add walnuts and toss to coat evenly.

*Add 1 tablespoon vinegar or lemon juice to regular milk to sour it
if buttermilk is not available.*

Citrus Pound Cake

12 – 16 servings

A light moist cake with a citrus twist.

1 cup	butter, softened
¼ cup	shortening
2 cups	sugar
5	eggs, at room temperature
3 cups	flour
½ teaspoon	salt
½ teaspoon	baking soda
½ teaspoon	baking powder
1 cup	buttermilk, at room temperature
1 teaspoon	vanilla extract
1 teaspoon	lemon extract

Glaze

2½ teaspoons	orange zest
2½ teaspoons	lemon zest
3 tablespoons	freshly squeezed orange juice
3 tablespoons	freshly squeezed lemon juice
1 cup	powdered sugar

Preheat oven to 325 degrees. Grease and flour a 10-inch tube or bundt pan. Cream butter, shortening and sugar until light and fluffy. Add eggs, one at a time, beating well after each addition. Combine flour, salt, baking soda and baking powder and add to creamed mixture alternately with buttermilk, ending with dry ingredients. Beat well after each addition. Add vanilla and lemon extracts. Spoon batter into prepared pan. Bake for 45 to 60 minutes or until a toothpick inserted in the center comes out dry and clean. Meanwhile, make glaze by combining orange and lemon zests, orange and lemon juices and powdered sugar, blending until smooth. Set aside. Cool cake on wire rack for 15 minutes before removing from pan. Place cake on wire rack to cool further. Punch holes in warm cake with toothpick and drizzle glaze over cake repeatedly until absorbed.

Raisin Spice Cake

Serves 8 – 10

1 cup	**raisins**
3 cups	**boiling water**
½ cup	**butter or margarine**
1 cup	**brown sugar**
1	**egg**
1¾ cups	**flour**
1 teaspoon	**baking soda**
1 teaspoon	**cinnamon**
1 teaspoon	**ground cloves**
½ teaspoon	**nutmeg**

Preheat oven to 350 degrees. Boil raisins and water together until 1 cup of liquid is left, approximately 15 minutes. Drain, reserving liquid. Cream butter and sugar until light and fluffy and add egg. Set aside. Combine flour, baking soda, cinnamon, cloves and nutmeg. Add dry ingredients to butter and sugar mixture alternately with raisin liquid, beating well after each addition. Stir in raisins. Pour into a greased and floured 8 x 8-inch pan. Bake for 35 to 40 minutes.

Toffee Cake

This cake melts in your mouth!

2 cups	brown sugar
2 cups	flour
½ cup	butter or margarine
1	egg
1 cup	milk
1 teaspoon	salt
½ teaspoon	baking soda
1 teaspoon	vanilla
6	toffee candy bars, frozen (such as Heath Bars)
½ cup	pecans, chopped

Preheat oven to 350 degrees. Combine sugar and flour. Cut in butter until the mixture resembles corn meal. Reserve one cup of this mixture. To remaining mixture, add egg, milk, salt, baking soda, and vanilla. Beat well. Pour into greased and floured 9 x 13-inch pan. Chop frozen candy bars into small pieces. (Place candy in a plastic bag, then break into bits with a hammer.) Blend candy bits with chopped pecans and 1 cup reserved crumb mixture. Spread evenly on top of cake batter. Bake for 35 minutes. Cool in pan on a wire rack.

Fresh Banana Cheesecake

Crust

1½ cups	quick-cooking rolled oats
½ cup	pecans, finely chopped
½ cup	brown sugar
⅓ cup	butter, melted

Preheat oven to 350 degrees. Stir together oats, pecans, brown sugar and butter until well combined. Press firmly into the bottom and sides of a 9-inch springform pan. Bake for 18 minutes or until golden brown. Cool.

Filling

1 pound	cream cheese, at room temperature
1 cup	ripe bananas, mashed
¾ cup	sugar
2 teaspoons	lemon juice
4	eggs

Topping

1 cup	sour cream
2 tablespoons	sugar
1 teaspoon	vanilla
Garnish:	*Banana slices*

Preheat oven to 350 degrees. Beat together cream cheese, bananas, ¾ cup sugar and lemon juice until well blended. Add eggs, one at a time, beating well after each addition. Pour into crust. Bake for 40 minutes. While cake is baking, prepare sour cream topping by mixing together sour cream, 2 tablespoons sugar and vanilla until well blended. Remove cheesecake from oven and top with sour cream mixture. Return to oven and bake for 10 minutes more. Cool slightly. Loosen cake from sides of pan. Cool to room temperature. Refrigerate uncovered overnight. Garnish with banana slices before serving.

Carrot Cake
With Dried Fruit

Serves 12

½ cup	dried apricots, chopped
½ cup	dried peaches, chopped
½ cup	dried Calymyrna figs,* chopped
3 tablespoons	bourbon
1 cup	unsalted butter, cut into 8 pieces, softened
1½ cups	sugar
3 large	eggs, at room temperature
2 teaspoons	vanilla extract
1¾ cups	sifted flour
2 teaspoons	baking powder
2 teaspoons	cinnamon
½ teaspoon	salt
¼ teaspoon	nutmeg
¼ teaspoon	mace
¼ teaspoon	allspice
¾ cup	pecans, coarsely chopped
2	large carrots, peeled and shredded
1 tablespoon	powdered sugar

Combine dried fruits and bourbon in a medium bowl and let stand 2 hours, stirring occasionally. (Or microwave, uncovered, on high, until fruits are plumped. Stir well.) Preheat oven to 350 degrees. Butter and flour a 12-cup bundt pan. In a large bowl, cream butter and sugar until light and fluffy. Add eggs and vanilla and blend thoroughly. Sift together flour, baking powder, cinnamon, salt, nutmeg, mace and allspice in a separate bowl. Stir in pecans. Mix carrots with dried fruit mixture. Add ¼ cup dry ingredients and toss to coat, separating fruit pieces. Stir fruit mixture gently into egg mixture, and fold in remaining dry ingredients. Transfer batter to bundt pan. Bake

continued...

until tester inserted near the center of the cake comes out clean, approximately 45 minutes. Cool cake in pan on rack for 10 minutes. Turn cake out onto rack to cool completely. Sift powdered sugar over cake before serving.

Chocolate Crunch

Serves 10 – 12

¾ cup	butter, melted
4 cups	vanilla wafers, coarsely chopped
2 cups	walnuts, chopped
6	eggs, separated
2 cups	powdered sugar, sifted
½ cup	butter
4 teaspoons	vanilla
pinch	salt
3 ounces	unsweetened chocolate, melted
½ cup	Creme de Cacao
½ cup	whipped cream

Combine melted butter, vanilla wafer pieces and walnuts. Set aside. Beat egg yolks, powdered sugar, butter, vanilla and salt until light and fluffy. Blend in melted chocolate. In a separate bowl, beat egg whites until stiff. Fold egg whites into chocolate mixture. Press half of the cookie mixture into a 9 x 13-inch pan. Pour chocolate mixture over cookie layer and top with remaining half of cookie mixture. Press topping down gently into the liquid layer and freeze. When frozen, top with Creme de Cacao. Serve with a dollop of whipped cream.

Apple Grand Tortoni *Serves 12 – 16*

Crust

1 cup	butter
⅔ cup	sugar
½ teaspoon	vanilla
2 cups	flour

Cream butter and sugar until light and fluffy. Add vanilla and flour. Blend well. Press mixture into the bottom and three-fourths of the way up the sides of a deep 9-inch springform pan.

Filling

8 ounces	cream cheese, softened
¼ cup	sugar
1 teaspoon	vanilla
1	egg
3 to 4	apples, peeled and thinly sliced
⅓ cup	sugar
1 teaspoon	cinnamon
1 tablespoon	lemon juice
¼ cup	almonds, sliced

Preheat oven to 450 degrees. Beat cream cheese, ¼ cup sugar, vanilla, and egg. Pour over crust. Mix apples with sugar, cinnamon, and lemon juice. Pour apple mixture on top of cheese mixture and sprinkle with sliced almonds. Using a wooden spoon, push crust down on sides even with apples. Bake at 450 degrees for 10 minutes, then at 400 degrees for 25 minutes. Serve warm or chilled.

Note: Number of apples needed may vary depending on their size.

Deluxe Carrot Cake

Serves 10 – 12

This three-layer cake is as delicious as it is beautiful!

2 cups	flour
2 cups	sugar
2 teaspoons	baking soda
1 teaspoon	salt
2 teaspoons	cinnamon
4	eggs
1 cup	vegetable oil
4 cups	carrots, grated
¾ cup	macadamia nuts,* chopped

Preheat oven to 350 degrees. Combine flour, sugar, baking soda, salt, and cinnamon. Set aside. In a large bowl, beat eggs until foamy. Slowly beat in oil. Add flour mixture gradually, beating until smooth. Mix in carrots and nuts. Pour into 3 greased and floured 9-inch round cake pans. Bake for 25 minutes. Cool for 10 minutes before removing from pans. Then cool completely on racks. Frost with Coconut Cream Cheese Frosting.

Coconut Cream Cheese Frosting

4 tablespoons	butter or margarine, divided
2 cups	coconut*
8 ounces	cream cheese
2 teaspoons	milk
3½ cups	powdered sugar, sifted
½ teaspoon	vanilla

Melt 2 tablespoons butter in a skillet. Add coconut and cook, stirring constantly over low heat, until golden brown. Cool on paper towels. Cream remaining 2 tablespoons butter and cream cheese. Add milk and sugar alternately, beating well after each addition. Add vanilla and stir in 1¾ cups of the prepared coconut. Frost each layer and sprinkle top with remaining coconut.

Chocolate Indulgence

Serves 8 – 10

8 ounces	**semi-sweet or bittersweet chocolate**
4 ounces	**unsalted butter**
5	**eggs, separated**
⅔ cup *plus*	
¼ cup	**sugar, divided**
	powdered sugar

Preheat oven to 325 degrees. Butter and flour a 9-inch springform pan. Cut chocolate and butter into large pieces and melt together over low heat, stirring frequently. Let cool slightly. In a large bowl, whisk egg yolks with ⅔ cup sugar. Stir in melted chocolate and butter, combining well. Set aside. Beat egg whites until soft peaks form. Slowly beat in ¼ cup sugar until whites hold stiff, glossy peaks. Add approximately one fourth of the egg whites to the chocolate mixture and mix well. Fold in remaining egg whites. Pour into prepared pan and bake for 1 hour or until tester inserted in center of cake comes out dry. Let cool for 1 hour and remove sides of pan. The center of the cake will fall as it cools. Dust with powdered sugar before serving. Note: If cake is not served warm, let stand in refrigerator for at least four hours, wrapped in foil, before serving.

Use cocoa powder to coat bottom and sides of pan instead of flour so that outside of cake remains dark when removed from pan.

Mocha Cheesecake

Serves 10 – 12

1 cup	graham cracker crumbs
¼ cup	butter
2 tablespoons	sugar
½ teaspoon	cinnamon
2 tablespoons	instant coffee
¼ cup	hot water
1½ pounds	cream cheese, at room temperature
¾ cup	sugar
3 large	eggs
8 ounces	semi-sweet chocolate
2 tablespoons	whipping cream
1 cup	sour cream
¼ cup	coffee liqueur
2 teaspoons	vanilla
Garnish:	Chocolate shavings

Preheat oven to 350 degrees. Butter sides of 8-inch springform pan. Combine graham cracker crumbs, butter, sugar and cinnamon. Press evenly onto bottom of pan. Chill while making filling. Dissolve instant coffee in hot water. Set aside to cool. Beat cream cheese until smooth. Add sugar gradually, mixing until well blended. Add eggs one at a time, beating well after each addition. Melt chocolate with whipping cream over low heat, stirring constantly. Add to cheese mixture, blending well. Mix in sour cream, then cooled coffee and liqueur. Beat in vanilla. Pour over prepared crust. Bake for 45 minutes or until sides are slightly puffed. Center will be still a bit soft, but will firm up when chilled. Cool cake on rack. Refrigerate, uncovered, for at least 12 hours before serving. Garnish with chocolate shavings and serve.

Irish Cream Cheesecake   *Serves 12 – 16*

Crust

10	graham crackers, broken
5 ounces	pecans
¼ cup	sugar
6 tablespoons	unsalted butter, melted

Lightly butter a 9-inch springform pan with 2¾-inch sides. Finely grind graham crackers, pecans and sugar in food processor. Add butter and blend. Press crumbs on bottom and 2 inches up sides of prepared pan. Refrigerate for 20 minutes.

Filling

1½ pounds	cream cheese, at room temperature
¾ cup	sugar
3 large	eggs
⅓ cup	Irish cream liqueur
1 teaspoon	vanilla
3 ounces	white chocolate, broken into pieces

Preheat oven to 325 degrees. Beat cream cheese and sugar in a large bowl until smooth and creamy. Whisk eggs, liqueur and vanilla until just blended. Add to cream cheese mixture and beat thoroughly. Finely chop white chocolate in food processor using on/off pulses. Stir into cream cheese mixture. Pour filling into crust. Bake until edges of filling are puffed and dry and center is just set, about 50 minutes. Cool on rack.

Topping

1½ cups	sour cream
¼ cup	powdered sugar
1½ ounces	white chocolate, grated
24	pecan halves

continued...

Mix sour cream and powdered sugar in a small bowl until smooth. Spread topping on cooled cake. Refrigerate for 6 hours, until chilled. Sprinkle cake with grated chocolate. Place pecan halves around edge and serve.

Jack O'Lantern Cheesecake

Serves 12 – 16

Serve this instead of the traditional pumpkin pie during the holiday season.

2 cups	**gingersnaps, crushed**
1 cup	**sugar, divided**
6 – 8 tablespoons	**butter, melted**
1½ pounds	**cream cheese, at room temperature**
¾ cup	**light brown sugar**
5	**eggs**
1 (16-ounce) can	**solid pack pumpkin**
1½ tablespoons	**pumpkin pie spice**
¼ cup	**heavy whipping cream**

Preheat oven to 325 degrees. Blend gingersnap crumbs and ¼ cup sugar with enough butter to moisten. Press mixture into the bottom and sides of a lightly buttered 9-inch springform pan. Chill while preparing filling. Beat cream cheese until smooth. Gradually blend in remaining sugar and brown sugar. Beat until combined. Add eggs, one at a time, beating well after each addition. Stir in pumpkin, pumpkin pie spice and cream. Pour into crust. Bake for 1 hour and 45 minutes or until center no longer looks wet or shiny. Cool on rack. Refrigerate overnight before serving.

Beautiful Amaretto Cheesecake

Serves 12 – 16

Rich and elegant.

Crust

1 cup	flour
6 tablespoons	butter
½ cup	sugar
½ cup	semi-sweet chocolate chips, melted

Preheat oven to 300 degrees. Combine flour, butter, sugar and melted chocolate in a food processor until mixture resembles dry pie crust. Press onto bottom and about 1 inch up sides of a 9-inch springform pan. Bake for 10 minutes.

Filling

1½ pounds	cream cheese, at room temperature
5	eggs
1 cup	sugar
1 cup	semi-sweet chocolate chips, melted
½ cup	Amaretto, divided
½ teaspoon	almond extract

Topping

1 pint	sour cream
4 tablespoons	sugar

Beat cream cheese until smooth. Add eggs one at a time, beating after each addition. Add 1 cup sugar and beat well. Beat in ¼ cup Amaretto and almond extract. Remove ⅔ of this batter and put into a small bowl. Set aside. Add melted chocolate and remaining ¼ cup Amaretto to remaining batter. Mix well. Pour half of the plain batter into the crust. Pour the chocolate batter in dollops on top of this. Top with remaining plain batter. Without

continued...

disturbing the crust, draw a small spatula or knife through the filling to create a marbled effect. Bake for 2 hours. Remove from oven and let rest for 10 minutes. Do not turn off oven. Meanwhile, combine sour cream and 4 tablespoons sugar. After cheesecake has cooled for 10 minutes, top with sour cream and sugar mixture and return to oven. Bake for 5 more minutes. Cool cake on a rack. Refrigerate uncovered overnight. Garnish (if desired) and serve.

Garnish: *½ ounce unsweetened chocolate (optional)*

Melt the chocolate over low heat. Prepare a paper cone out of waxed or parchment paper. Place melted chocolate in cone and fold the two sides of the cone towards the middle. Fold the top down to enclose the chocolate. Cut off tip of cone and pipe chocolate onto top of cake in a back and forth swirled pattern. Draw a toothpick lightly through the piped chocolate to make a design.

Cheesecake 'Alani

A cheesecake with a hint of orange.

Crust

1 cup	**sifted flour**
¼ cup	**sugar**
1 tablespoon	**orange zest**
½ cup	**butter**
1	**egg yolk**
½ teaspoon	**vanilla**

Preheat oven to 400 degrees. Combine flour, sugar and orange zest. Cut in butter until mixture resembles coarse meal. Blend in the egg yolk and vanilla thoroughly. Pat half of the dough evenly over the bottom of a 10-inch springform pan. Bake for 5 minutes. When pan has cooled, pat remaining dough evenly around sides of pan to within ½ inch of the top. Set aside and prepare filling.

Filling

2½ pounds	**cream cheese, at room temperature**
1 ¾ cups	**sugar**
3 tablespoons	**flour**
1 tablespoon	**orange zest**
¼ teaspoon	**salt**
¼ teaspoon	**vanilla**
5	**eggs**
¼ cup	**frozen orange juice concentrate, thawed**
Garnish:	*Orange slices*

continued...

Combine cream cheese, sugar, flour, orange zest, salt, vanilla and eggs. Beat until smooth. Stir in orange juice. Pour filling into prepared crust. Place cheesecake on a cookie sheet and bake for 8 to 10 minutes. Lower temperature to 225 degrees and bake for 2 hours or until center no longer looks wet or shiny. Cool to room temperature. Refrigerate uncovered, overnight. Garnish with orange slices before serving.

Cheesecakes shrink as they cool. If the filling sticks to the side of the pan, it may crack. To prevent this, run a knife around the edge of the cheesecake to separate it from the pan after removing it from the oven.

Crustless Cranberry Pie

Serves 8

Freeze fresh cranberries to prepare this tart pie out of season.

10 ounces	**cranberries**
1¼ cups	**sugar, divided**
½ cup	**macadamia nuts,* diced**
2	**eggs**
¾ cup	**flour**
¼ cup	**butter, melted**
¼ cup	**vegetable oil**

Preheat oven to 325 degrees. Spread cranberries in a well-greased 9-inch pie plate. Sprinkle cranberries with ½ cup sugar and macadamia nuts. Beat eggs, gradually adding remaining ¾ cup sugar. Add flour, butter, and vegetable oil and beat well. Pour mixture over cranberries and bake for 60 minutes. Serve warm or cold.

Frosted Kiwi Tart

Serves 8 – 10

Crust

1 cup	**vanilla wafer crumbs**
2 tablespoons	**butter, melted**

Mix vanilla wafer crumbs and melted butter. Press firmly onto the bottom of a 9-inch pie or tart plate. Freeze.

Filling

1¼ cups	**kiwi fruit puree**
½ cup	**water**
⅓ cup	**sugar**
2 tablespoons	**light corn syrup**
	juice and zest of 1 lemon
Garnish:	*Lemon slices*

Combine kiwi fruit puree, water, sugar, syrup, lemon juice and lemon zest. Pour into a 9-inch square pan and freeze until firm but not solid, about 1½ hours. Transfer mixture to a chilled bowl and beat until light but still frozen. Spoon into frozen crust. Return to freezer and freeze for at least 4 hours. Garnish with lemon slices.

Note: The kiwi puree mixture may also be served, without the crust, as a sorbet.

Lemon Ribbon Pie

Serves 8

A cool and creamy summertime treat.

1 (9-inch)	pie shell, baked
1 quart	vanilla ice cream, softened
6 tablespoons	butter
	zest of 1 lemon
⅓ cup	lemon juice
⅛ teaspoon	salt
1 cup *plus* 6 tablespoons	sugar, divided
2	eggs
2	egg yolks
3	egg whites

Smooth half of the ice cream into the pie shell. Freeze. Melt butter in a saucepan over low heat. Add lemon zest, lemon juice, salt and 1 cup sugar and mix well. Slightly beat eggs with egg yolks. Combine with lemon juice mixture and cook over low heat, beating constantly with a wire whisk until smooth, approximately 10 to 15 minutes. Let cool. Spread ice cream with half of the lemon butter sauce and freeze until firm. Spread with the remaining ice cream and freeze. Top with remaining lemon butter sauce and freeze. Preheat oven to 475 degrees. Beat egg whites until they form soft peaks. Gradually beat in 6 tablespoons sugar until whites are thick and glossy. Spread meringue on the pie. Place on cookie sheet in oven and bake until lightly browned on top. Serve immediately.

Chocolate Chip Pecan Pie *Serves 8*

Crust

⅓ cup *plus* 1 tablespoon	shortening
1 cup	flour
½ teaspoon	salt
2 – 3 tablespoons	ice water

Preheat oven to 475 degrees. Cut shortening into flour and salt until mixture resembles coarse crumbs. Stir in the water, 1 tablespoon at a time, until the dough holds together. Form pastry into a rough ball and shape into flat disk on a lightly floured surface. Roll pastry from center to the edge until it is about ⅛ inch thick and 1½ to 2 inches larger than the pie plate. Fit the crust into a 9-inch pie plate, pressing firmly against bottom and side. Prick bottom and sides of pastry with fork. Bake for 5 minutes.

Filling

¾ cup	brown sugar
¼ teaspoon	salt
1¼ cups	dark corn syrup
3 teaspoons	butter, melted
3	eggs
1 teaspoon	vanilla
1 cup	pecans, coarsely chopped
6 ounces	semi-sweet chocolate chips
½ cup	pecan halves

continued...

Reduce oven temperature to 350 degrees. Combine sugar, salt, corn syrup, butter, eggs and vanilla in a large bowl and beat until well blended. Stir in chopped pecans and chocolate chips. Pour into crust. Distribute pecan halves on top. Bake for 40 to 50 minutes. Cool to room temperature. Filling will set and firm as it cools. Serve at room temperature or chilled with sweetened whipped cream.

Topping

1 cup	**whipping cream**
3 tablespoons	**sugar**
1 teaspoon	**vanilla extract**

Beat cream with sugar and vanilla until stiff.

Note: For a mocha variation, omit vanilla extract and add ½ teaspoon instant coffee.

Mango Cream Cheese Pie

Crust

2 cups	sifted flour
½ cup	powdered sugar, sifted
¾ cup	butter

Preheat oven to 350 degrees. Combine flour and sugar and cut in butter. Press into bottom of a 9 x 13-inch pan. Bake for 20 to 25 minutes or until light brown. Cool.

Cream Cheese Layer

8 ounces	cream cheese
½ cup	sugar
1 teaspoon	vanilla
½ cup	whipping cream
1 tablespoon	sugar

Beat cream cheese and ½ cup sugar until light and fluffy. Set aside. Beat whipping cream with 1 tablespoon sugar and vanilla until stiff. Fold into cream cheese mixture. Spread over cooled crust and chill until firm.

Mango Layer

2 envelopes	unflavored gelatin
1 cup	cold water
1 cup	boiling water
1 cup	sugar
5 cups	mangoes* or peaches, peeled, diced and drained

continued...

Sprinkle gelatin over cold water to soften. Add boiling water and sugar. Mix well. Let cool. Stir in mangoes. Chill until slightly thickened. Pour fruit mixture over cream cheese layer and chill until firm.

Note: Ripeness of mangoes will determine the amount of sugar needed. Use less sugar with riper mangoes.

Super Lemon Bars   *Makes 2½ dozen*

Crust

2 cups	flour
½ cup	macadamia nuts,* finely chopped
½ cup	powdered sugar
1 cup	butter

Preheat oven to 350 degrees. Combine flour, macadamia nuts, powdered sugar and butter. Press into a greased 9 x 13-inch pan and bake for 20 to 25 minutes until golden brown.

Filling

¼ cup	flour
½ teaspoon	baking powder
4	eggs
2 cups	sugar
½ cup	lemon juice
1 teaspoon	lemon zest (optional)
	powdered sugar

Combine flour, baking powder, eggs, sugar, lemon juice and lemon zest. Mix well. Spread over baked crust. Bake until set, about 25 minutes. Cool. Dust top with sifted powdered sugar and cut into 3 x 1-inch bars.

Sunny Cookies

Makes 5 – 6 dozen

1 cup	sugar
¾ cup	brown sugar
1 cup	shortening
2	eggs
1 teaspoon	vanilla
2 cups	flour
½ teaspoon	baking powder
1 teaspoon	baking soda
¼ teaspoon	salt
2 cups	quick-cooking rolled oats
¾ cup	coconut*
¾ cup	sunflower seeds, unsalted
	sugar

Preheat oven to 350 degrees. Cream sugars, shortening, eggs, and vanilla. Add flour, baking powder, baking soda, and salt. Mix well. Stir in oatmeal, coconut, and sunflower seeds. Take teaspoonfuls of dough and shape into balls. Roll in sugar and bake on greased cookie sheet for 10 to 12 minutes or until lightly browned.

Crunchy Jumble Cookies

Makes 3 – 4 dozen

These cookies contain a little bit of everything!

½ cup	butter or margarine
1 cup	sugar
1	egg
1 teaspoon	vanilla
1¼ cups	flour
½ teaspoon	baking soda
¼ teaspoon	salt
1 (6-ounce) package	semi-sweet chocolate chips
½ cup	walnuts, chopped
1 cup	raisins
2 cups	crispy rice cereal

Preheat oven to 350 degrees. Cream butter and sugar until light and fluffy. Blend in egg and vanilla. Add flour, baking soda, and salt and mix well. Stir in chocolate chips, walnuts, raisins, and rice cereal. Shape dough by heaping tablespoons into balls. Place about 2 inches apart on ungreased cookie sheet. Flatten slightly. Bake for 12 to 14 minutes.

Oatmeal Chewies

Makes 5 dozen

1 cup	butter
1 cup	sugar
1 cup	brown sugar
2	eggs
1 teaspoon	vanilla
1½ cups	flour
1 teaspoon	salt
1 teaspoon	baking soda
3 cups	quick-cooking rolled oats
2 cups	raisins

Preheat oven to 350 degrees. Cream butter and sugars. Add eggs and vanilla and beat well. Add flour, salt and baking soda, mixing well. Stir in oatmeal and raisins. Shape dough into 1-inch balls. Place about 3 inches apart on ungreased cookie sheet. Flatten slightly. Bake for 10 to 12 minutes or until medium brown. Cool for 1 minute before removing from cookie sheet. Cool completely.

Lots of Chocolate Chips Cookies

Makes 7– 8 dozen

2 cups	sugar
2 cups	brown sugar
1 cup	margarine, softened
1 cup	unsalted butter, softened
3	eggs, at room temperature
2 teaspoons	baking powder
1 teaspoon	baking soda
1 teaspoon	salt
2 teaspoons	vanilla
3 cups	flour
2 cups	oat flour, made by putting 3 cups oatmeal in blender and pulverizing it
3 (6-ounce) packages	semi-sweet chocolate chips
2 cups	walnuts, chopped (optional)

Cream sugars, margarine and butter. Add eggs, one at a time, beating well after each addition. Add baking powder, baking soda, salt and vanilla to the creamed mixture. Stir in flour and oat flour. Add chocolate chips and walnuts, stirring by hand. Dough will be thick. Refrigerate overnight. Preheat oven to 400 degrees. Drop dough by rounded teaspoonfuls about 2 inches apart onto greased cookie sheet. Bake until medium brown, about 6 to 8 minutes. Cool on cookie sheets for 2 minutes before transferring to wire racks.

Pecan Thins
Makes 7 dozen

Light and elegant dessert cookies.

1 cup	**unsalted butter, softened**
¾ cup	**sugar**
1	**egg**
1 teaspoon	**vanilla**
1¾ cups	**unsifted flour**
	pecan halves

Preheat oven to 350 degrees. Beat butter, eggs, sugar and vanilla until light and fluffy. Add flour, beating until just combined. Drop dough by level teaspoonfuls, 2 inches apart, onto ungreased cookie sheets. Press pecan halves lightly down in the center of each cookie. Bake 8 to 10 minutes, or until edges of the cookies are golden brown. Let cool 1 minute, then transfer to wire racks to cool completely.

Quick and Easy Brownies
Makes 1½ dozen

2 ounces	**unsweetened chocolate**
¼ pound	**butter**
1 cup	**sugar**
2	**eggs**
½ teaspoon	**vanilla**
¼ cup	**flour**
¼ teaspoon	**salt**
1 cup	**walnuts, chopped**

Preheat oven to 350 degrees. Melt chocolate and butter in a heavy saucepan over low heat. Remove from heat and add sugar. Add eggs and vanilla. Beat well. Stir in flour, salt and walnuts. Pour into a greased 8 x 8-inch pan and bake for 40 minutes. Cool. Cut into 2-inch squares.

Brownies
Hawaiian Style

Makes 4 dozen

4 ounces	**unsweetened chocolate**
½ cup	**butter**
4	**eggs**
1 cup	**sugar**
2 teaspoons	**vanilla**
1 cup	**flour**
1 cup	**macadamia nuts,* chopped**
1 (12-ounce) package	**semi-sweet chocolate chips**
1 (7-ounce) package	**shredded coconut***

Preheat oven to 350 degrees. Melt chocolate and butter in a heavy saucepan over low heat. Cool. Beat eggs until foamy. Gradually beat sugar and vanilla into eggs. Blend in chocolate mixture. Add flour and mix until combined. Stir in half of the macadamia nuts, chocolate chips and coconut. Pour into a greased 9 x 13-inch baking pan and bake for 25 minutes or until brownies pull away from sides of pan. Remove from oven and spread remaining macadamia nuts, chocolate chips and coconut on top. Return to oven and bake for 10 more minutes. Cool. Cut into 1½-inch squares.

For healthier brownies from a packaged mix, substitute ½ cup non-fat or low-fat plain yogurt for oil and eggs.

Crunchy Chunky Chocolate Cookies

Makes 1½ dozen

4 ounces	unsweetened chocolate
1⅓ cups	sugar
½ cup	butter, softened
2	eggs
1 tablespoon	instant coffee
1 tablespoon	vanilla extract
1 cup	flour
½ teaspoon	salt
2 cups	semi-sweet chocolate chips
1 cup	walnuts, coarsely chopped

Preheat oven to 350 degrees. Melt chocolate in a heavy saucepan over low heat, stirring constantly. Set aside to cool. Cream butter and sugar until light and fluffy. Add eggs, one at a time, beating well after each addition. Add coffee and vanilla and blend until fluffy. Stir in melted chocolate. Add flour and salt and mix just until combined. Stir in chocolate chips and nuts. Drop dough by ¼ cupfuls, 2 inches apart, onto greased cookie sheets. Bake cookies until they look dry and centers are still slightly soft to the touch, about 15 minutes. Cool on cookie sheet for 5 minutes. Transfer to rack and cool completely.

Kissed Peanut Butter Cookies

Makes 4 dozen

½ cup	sugar
½ cup	brown sugar
½ cup	butter or shortening
½ cup	peanut butter
1	egg
2 tablespoons	milk
1 teaspoon	vanilla
1¾ cups	flour
1 teaspoon	baking soda
½ teaspoon	salt
48	milk chocolate kisses

Preheat oven to 350 degrees. Mix sugars, butter, peanut butter, egg, milk and vanilla. Stir in flour, baking soda and salt. Form into 1-inch balls. Place on a greased cookie sheet and bake for 8 minutes. Remove from oven and press a chocolate kiss into the center of each cookie. Return to oven and bake an additional 2 to 3 minutes. Watch the cookies to make sure that the kisses get warm enough to fuse to the cookies, but do not melt. Cool on cookie sheets until firm.

Carrot Cookies

Makes 4 dozen

¾ cup	butter or margarine, softened
¾ cup	brown sugar
½ cup	sugar
1	egg
1 teaspoon	vanilla
1¾ cups	flour
1 teaspoon	baking powder
½ teaspoon	baking soda
½ teaspoon	cinnamon
¼ teaspoon	ground cloves
2 cups	quick-cooking rolled oats
1 cup	carrots, shredded
½ cup	raisins
½ cup	pecans, chopped

Preheat oven to 375 degrees. Beat butter and sugars until light and fluffy. Beat in egg and vanilla. Stir in flour, baking powder, baking soda, cinnamon and ground cloves. Mix well. Stir in oats, carrots, raisins and pecans. Drop dough by rounded teaspoonfuls, about 2 inches apart, onto ungreased cookie sheet. Bake for 10 to 12 minutes. Cool on cookie sheet before transferring to wire rack.

Cereal Crisps

Makes 3 dozen

1 cup	butter
1 cup	sugar
2 teaspoons	vanilla
1	egg
1½ cups	flour
1 teaspoon	baking soda
½ teaspoon	salt
2 cups	flaked rice cereal
	flaked rice cereal for rolling

Preheat oven to 375 degrees. Combine flour, soda and salt in a small bowl and set aside. Beat butter and sugar until light and creamy, then add vanilla. Add egg and beat well. Sift together flour, baking soda and salt and add to batter. Stir in 2 cups cereal. Shape dough by teaspoonfuls into balls and roll in cereal. Place on an ungreased cookie sheet and flatten slightly. Bake for 12 minutes.

Biscotti

Makes 1½ dozen

Traditional Italian dunking cookie.

2¼ cups	flour
1¼ cups	sugar
¼ teaspoon	baking powder
⅛ teaspoon	salt
3	eggs
1 tablespoon	vegetable oil
¼ teaspoon	vanilla extract
½ cup	macadamia nuts,* coarsely chopped
½ cup	semi-sweet chocolate chips (optional)
½ cup	grated coconut* (optional)

Preheat oven to 350 degrees. In a large bowl, sift together flour, sugar, baking powder and salt. Add eggs, oil and vanilla and mix well. Stir in macadamia nuts, chocolate chips and coconut. Dough will be very firm and sticky. Divide dough in half. On a lightly floured surface, shape dough into 2 flat bottomed cylinders measuring 8 inches long, 2½ inches wide and 1 inch high. Keep your hands floured to shape the dough. Place dough on a lightly greased cookie sheet. Bake for 25 to 30 minutes or until lightly browned on top. Remove from oven and let cool slightly. Remove cylinders from cookie sheet and place on a cutting board. Cut diagonally into ¾-inch slices. Place slices, cut side down, on a clean, dry cookie sheet. Return to the oven and bake an additional 15 minutes or until sides are golden. Cool on a wire rack, then transfer to an airtight container.

My Mom's Uncooked Fudge

Makes 16 pieces

4 ounces	unsweetened chocolate
½ cup	butter or margarine
1	egg
1 pound	powdered sugar, sifted
¼ cup	sweetened condensed milk
1 teaspoon	vanilla
½ cup	macadamia nuts,* chopped (optional)

Line an 8 x 8 x 2-inch pan with foil and grease it. Melt the chocolate and butter over low heat and mix well. Combine the egg, sugar, milk, and vanilla in a separate bowl and blend well. Stir in chocolate and butter mixture. Pour mixture into prepared pan and chill in refrigerator until set, approximately 30 minutes. Cut into bite-size pieces and serve.

Frosted Peanut Butter Bars

Serves 24

Sinfully rich and delicious.

1 cup	sugar
1 cup	light corn syrup
1 cup	peanut butter
6 cups	crispy rice cereal
1 (12-ounce) package	semi-sweet chocolate chips
1 (12-ounce) package	butterscotch chips

Grease a 9 x 13-inch pan. Combine sugar and corn syrup in a saucepan and bring to a boil. Add peanut butter and mix well. Remove from heat and add cereal. Mix until evenly coated. Press into pan. Set aside. Reserve ½ cup each chocolate chips and butterscotch chips. Melt remaining over low heat. Spread over cereal mixture. Let cool for 5 minutes, then sprinkle on reserved chips. Cut into squares.

Macadamia Nut Brittle

Makes 1 pound

Peanut brittle goes Hawaiian!

1 cup	sugar
½ cup	white corn syrup
¼ cup	water
¾ cup	whole macadamia nuts*
½ cup	macadamia nuts,* chopped
1 tablespoon	butter
½ teaspoon	vanilla
⅛ teaspoon	baking soda

Butter 2 cookie sheets. Place in a warm oven. Mix sugar, corn syrup and water in a saucepan. Cook over medium heat, stirring occasionally, until syrup reaches the soft-ball stage, 240 degrees on a candy thermometer. Stir in macadamia nuts and butter. Cook, stirring constantly, until thermometer reaches 300 degrees and syrup is brown in color. Remove from heat and stir in vanilla and baking soda. Pour half of the candy onto each cookie sheet and quickly spread about ¼-inch thick. When cool, break into pieces and store in a tightly covered tin.

Warming the cookie sheets helps the candy to spread into thin layers.

Macadamia Popcorn Crunch

7 cups	**popped popcorn**
1 (5-ounce) can	**macadamia nuts,* coarsely chopped**
¾ cup	**brown sugar**
⅓ cup	**margarine**
3 tablespoons	**light corn syrup**
¼ teaspoon	**vanilla**
¼ teaspoon	**baking soda**

Preheat oven to 300 degrees. Combine popcorn and macadamia nuts in a large, greased saucepan and place in oven while syrup is cooking. Combine brown sugar, margarine and corn syrup in a heavy saucepan over medium heat. Bring to a boil, stirring constantly with a wooden spoon. Boil for 4 minutes, stirring occasionally. The mixture should boil at a moderate rate over entire surface. Remove from heat. Stir in baking soda and vanilla. Pour over macadamia nuts and popcorn and stir until well coated. Bake for 10 minutes. Remove from oven and stir. Return to oven for another 5 minutes. Spread mixture onto aluminum foil to cool. Cool completely, then break up. Store in an airtight container.

Macadamia nuts were first brought to Hawai'i by William Purvis in 1882. The trees are medium sized with shiny, holly-like leaves. The white nuts are enclosed in a brittle shell which in turn is covered by a husk. The nuts fall to the ground when mature where they are gathered, dehusked, dried, and upon roasting, cracked open. Macadamia nuts are harvested from August to January. The peak season is October through November. Although some of the other islands have joined in the production of macadamia nuts, the island of Hawaii is still the largest commercial producer.

*In the islands, there's a lei for every occasion —
a tradition for students of hula — as standard as
a handshake for most politicians — or just a quiet
way to say 'thank you' to someone special.*

Glossary

Ahi

One of the most popular fish in Hawai'i. The name ahi applies to all the larger varieties of tuna found in Hawaiian waters, such as albacore, yellowfin, and big-eye tuna. Raw ahi is often used for sashimi. Ahi is most abundant from late spring through September.

Aku

Aku refers to the Skipjack Tuna and the Ocean Bonito. Aku is usually canned for export. When eaten raw, as sashimi, it has a surprisingly delicate flavor.

Arare

A seasoned Japanese rice cracker which comes in assorted shapes and sizes. Arare can be plain or garnished with seaweed or sesame seeds. It is a favorite local snack.

A'u

A'u is the Hawaiian name for marlin. This large billfish is tasty and lean. It is most abundant during the summer. A'u can be poached, fried, or marinated and then broiled. A'u may be substituted with shark or swordfish in most recipes.

Baby Corn

This is a tiny new ear of corn which comes canned.

Balsamic Vinegar

This dark brown vinegar comes from Modena, Italy. It requires six or more years to be processed and has a sweet-tart flavor.

Bamboo Shoots

Bamboo shoots or takenoko have a hearty, firm texture suitable for simmered dishes and one-pot cookery. The canned variety is widely used.

Bean Sprouts

Sprouted mung beans are available in markets and health food stores. Bean sprouts may be purchased fresh or canned.

Black Beans

Chinese black beans are cooked, salted and fermented soy beans. To prepare, rinse beans and then mash them with the back of a spoon.

Cajun Seasoning

Cajun seasoning is a blend of dried herbs and spices used in Cajun cooking, a combination of French and Southern Cuisines.

Calymyrna Figs

A variety of fig found in the United States. It has a rich flavor and is amber colored.

Canola Oil

Canola oil, made from rapeseed, has the lowest amount of saturated fat of any oil and the best fatty acid ratio. This flavorless oil has a very light color and a high smoking point.

Capers

The flower buds of the caper plant. This condiment is salted and preserved in vinegar.

Chili Oil

Oil flavored with hot chilies used as a seasoning in many Chinese dishes.

Chinese Noodles

*There are three main types of Chinese noodles. **Cellophane noodles** are thin, semi-transparent, flavorless noodles made*

312

*from ground mung beans. They are also called bean threads or bean noodles and may be deep fried or cooked in liquid. **Chinese egg noodles** (chow mein) are fine noodles that are similar in taste and appearance to regular egg noodles. They are made from wheat flour, water and egg. Chinese egg noodles are cooked in boiling water for a few minutes, just past the al dente stage. They may be deep fried in a nest shape, stir fried, added to soup or served with a sauce. Long uncut noodles are a symbol of longevity. **Rice sticks** are similar to cellophane noodles except they are made from rice flour. They are also called rice noodles or rice vermicelli.*

Chinese Parsley

A coriander spice plant which is also known as cilantro.

Chutney

A spicy condiment made with fruits, spices, sugar and vinegar. An accompaniment to meats and curried foods.

Coconut

The nut or fruit of a coconut palm tree. The creamy, white meat of the young coconut fruit can be easily removed with a spoon. The meat of the mature coconut is firm and is usually grated. Shredded and flaked coconut is available in cans or packages.

Coconut Milk

Coconut milk is made by simmering water and fresh coconut pulp. The mixture is then strained through a cheesecloth. Coconut milk is available frozen.

Coconut Syrup

Coconut syrup is made from coconut water, grated fresh coconut, sugar and cream of tartar.

Coconut Water

The liquid found in the center of a coconut. There are three eyes on the top of the coconut which can be opened to drain the liquid.

Da Kine

A catch-all phrase for miscellaneous items.

Daikon

Daikon is a common ingredient in Japanese cooking. It is in the turnip family though it is more radish-like in flavor. Any turnip may be used as a substitute.

Dijon Mustard

This condiment originated in Dijon, France. It is a combination of dry mustard, herbs, spices and white wine. Dijon mustard goes well with meats, fish, and poultry.

Dim Sum

Dim Sum are Chinese dumplings with wheat flour or glutenous rice dough wrappings that are filled with flavorful mixtures of pork, beef, fish or vegetables. Dim sum are steamed, baked or fried.

Feta Cheese

This cheese is made from ewe's milk or ewe's and goat's milk. It is a soft cheese with a sharp and salty flavor, which may be used in cooking.

Fish Sauce

An anchovy-based, dark sauce with a strong aroma used to flavor Southeast Asian food. Fish sauce is rich in B vitamins and protein.

Fontina Cheese

A semi-soft to hard cheese made with cow's milk. It has a light yellow color and a delicate nutty flavor.

Ginger

A gnarled light brown root with a pungent, spicy flavor. Peel, then slice, mince or grate for maximum flavor. To store, refrigerate in a jar of sherry or freeze in a plastic bag.

Gorgonzola Cheese

This cheese is made from cow's milk. It is semi-soft and has a color and texture similar to blue cheese.

Guava

A plum-sized tropical fruit. Guava is used primarily in juices, preserves, jellies, sauces and syrups, or eaten raw.

Guri-Guri

A sherbet-like dessert which originated on Maui.

Hawaiian Chili Pepper

A small, orange-red fruit used as a spicy seasoning.

Hoisin Sauce

A sweet fermented bean sauce. Hoisin sauce is made from soy beans with garlic, glutinous red rice, salt and sugar. It is used as a condiment with pork or roast duck and is often in marinades for poultry.

Hot Pepper Sauce

A watery, orange-red, bottled sauce that is used to add spicy hot seasoning to chili, seafood and sauces.

Inamona

A kukui nut paste that is used for flavoring in poke or as a condiment for other lu'au dishes. Also spelled inomono.

Italian Flat Leaf Parsley

A sweet, mild parsley that has a broad, flat leaf with jagged edges. Also known as Portuguese parsley.

Japanese Cucumber

This slender, elongated cucumber is crunchy and flavorful. It retains these qualities when combined with other ingredients better than the Western cucumber. The skin does not need to be peeled.

Japanese Eggplant

The Japanese eggplant is very dark purple and has a thin elongated shape. It is tender, almost seedless and requires little preparation.

Jicama

A brownish-gray skinned root vegetable resembling a turnip with crisp white sweet meat. It is sliced and eaten raw in salads or as a crudite, or cooked in stews. Lemon juice will keep raw jicama from turning brown. Jicama is sometimes called Chinese yam or Chop-suey yam.

Kalamata Olives

These superior Greek olives are purple-black and almond shaped. They can be found in specialty food stores. They are also known as calamata olives.

Kampyo

Dried gourd strips used in Asian cooking. Kampyo needs to be soaked or cooked before using. It is often found in Japanese sushi. Also spelled kanpyo.

Katakuri-Ko

This fine white powder is Japanese potato starch. It is used to keep fresh mochi (a sweet glutinous rice cake) from sticking together.

Ketjap Manis

A Javanese sauce made with soy sauce, palm syrup, garlic, star anise, salam leaves (a tropical laurel-like tree), and galangal (a relative of ginger). Ketjap manis is a fundamental ingredient in Javanese cooking.

Kona Coffee

Kona coffee is medium bodied, richly flavored and aromatic. It is grown on the southwest coast of the Big Island of Hawai'i.

Koshian

A smooth red bean paste mainly used in Japanese desserts.

Kula or Kahuku Tomatoes

Kula is an up-country town on the side of Haleakala, Maui, well known for its agricultural products such as Maui

316

onions, tomatoes and protea. Kahuku is a truck farming area on the North Shore of O'ahu, famous for corn, watermelon and prawns, as well as tomatoes.

Leeks

A member of the onion family, leeks have long, light green stalks with white bases. To prepare a leek for cooking, cut off the root end and the green tips so that five inches of the stalk remain. Remove the outer leaves. Wash thoroughly under running water to remove dirt and sand.

Lemon Grass

The fragrant gray-green lemon grass grows two feet long on a small bulbous base. The bottom six to eight inches of the stalk is used for cooking after the tough outer leaves are removed.

Light Soy Sauce

Soy sauce was invented by the Chinese who use both light and dark soy sauces. The light soy sauce does not contain molasses and is aged for a shorter period. Regular Japanese soy sauce may be substituted for light soy sauce in an emergency.

Lychee

A traditional Chinese fruit with a woody exterior surrounding a fleshy white sweet-flavored pulp. Fresh lychee may be frozen. Canned lychee is peeled and often seeded.

Macadamia Nuts

A member of the protea family, this nut is a delicacy. Macadamia nuts may be purchased whole, in pieces or in bits. For cooking, unsalted nuts are preferred. Macadamia nuts freeze well.

Mandarin Orange

A small yellow to red-orange citrus fruit whose family includes the tangerine, temple orange and Japanese satsuma orange. Canned mandarin oranges are the Satsuma variety from Japan.

Mango

This tropical fruit has a beautiful yellow color with splashes of red and orange. The fruit must be peeled and the fibrous seed removed before consumption. The best known varieties are Hayden, Pirie and Gouveia.

Manoa Lettuce

A leafy, semi-head lettuce also known as Green Mignonette, named after a verdant valley on the island of O'ahu. Any leafy green lettuce may be substituted.

Maui Onion

Sweet and mild, this is a Texas Bermuda Gravex Grano type onion grown in volcanic soil. A Texas onion or a Vidalia sweet onion can be substituted.

Mauna Kea

The tallest peak in the Pacific, Mauna Kea ("white mountain"), is located on the Island of Hawai'i. Measured from its base on the ocean floor, Mauna Kea is 31,796 feet tall, taller than Mt. Everest.

Mirin

A heavily sweetened rice wine used for flavoring or in marinades, mirin is an important ingredient in Japanese cooking. One teaspoon of sugar may be substituted for one teaspoon of mirin.

Miso

Miso is a fermented soy paste used in soups and stews. Aka miso is a dark red strongly flavored miso and shiro miso is a white, sweet, mildly flavored miso.

Mochiko

Sweet rice flour. Mochiko is the main ingredient in Japanese mochi (a sweet glutinous rice cake).

Nairagi

This striped marlin is an important billfish in the Hawaiian market and is found throughout the Indo-Pacific region. It is similar to the blue marlin and can be found as steaks or fillets at the fish market during the summer months.

Ogo

Ogo is a common name for limu manaea, a species of Hawaiian seaweed.

Old Bay Seasoning

A combination of seasonings for fish and seafood dishes popular on the East Coast.

Olive Oil

A flavorful oil used in many Italian dishes. Extra virgin olive oil is obtained from the first pressing of the olives and is recommended for its light, delicate flavor.

Onaga

This beautiful red fish is ranked near the top for taste among the snappers. Locally this red snapper can reach a size of thirty-six pounds, but more often it will range from one to fifteen pounds. It is available in the markets particularly around the New Year.

'Opakapaka

This popular Hawaiian fish is a pink snapper that is found in deep ocean water. It is most plentiful between October and January and weighs between three and ten pounds. 'Opakapaka meat is moist, has a mild delicate flavor and can be prepared in many ways. It blends well with other seafoods.

Opal Basil

A type of basil with crinkled purple leaves and pale pink flowers.

Oyster Sauce

A spiced concentrated liquid in which oysters have been cooked.

Panko

A Japanese crispy flour meal used for breading. Similar to coarse white bread crumbs.

Papaya

A pear or light-bulb-shaped yellow fruit with melon-like flesh. A ripe papaya has yellow skin with an occasional patch of green. It should be firm to touch. The skin is not eaten.

Papaya Seeds

These peppercorn-sized black seeds are found in the center of fresh papayas. To use papaya seeds in cooking, scoop out and rinse. Remove all the papaya flesh and fibers. Dry well. Ground papaya seeds impart a peppery flavor and are often used in salad dressings.

Parmesan Cheese

A hard cheese made from partly skimmed milk. The flavor intensifies with age. Whenever possible, use freshly grated Parmesan cheese.

Peanut Oil

A favorite oil in Chinese cooking, peanut oil can tolerate high temperatures without smoking. It is not likely to burn. Because it has a high smoke point, it does not pick up odors and flavors and may be strained and used again.

Pepperoncini

These mild, light green peppers are long and cone shaped. They are an essential ingredient in Italian antipasto. Pepperoncini is sometimes labeled as Greek peppers or sweet Italian peppers. It is also spelled pepperocini.

Pineapple

The pineapple is a pine-cone-shaped fruit with a horny rind that grows on a low cactus-like plant. Each plant produces one fruit every twenty to twenty-four months. The pineapple is native to South America.

Pickled Scallions

Otherwise known as rankyo or rakkyo, this Japanese condiment can be found in cans.

Plum Tomato

Small, oblong tomatoes that vine ripen to a deep red color.

They are firm and meaty, have few seeds, are low in acid and high in fruitiness.

Pupu

Finger food. Literally, a relish, snack or hors d'oeuvre.

Ramen Noodles

Dried ramen noodles are packaged in single serving cellophane bags. The noodles cook in boiling water for three minutes and come with a soup base seasoning packet. They are also called saimin noodles.

Rice Vinegar

Rice vinegar is made from fermented rice. It is lighter and sweeter than most Western vinegars. It is also called Japanese rice vinegar or Tamanoe vinegar.

Rice Wine

A Japanese wine known as sake, which is used in cooking and as a beverage. Dry sherry may be substituted.

Romano Cheese

A hard cheese made from cow's milk and aged for eight to twelve months. It has a salty, sharp taste and is grated for use in most recipes. Pecorino romano cheese is made with sheep's milk.

Saimin Noodles

Dried saimin noodles are packaged in single serving cellophane bags. The noodles cook in boiling water for three minutes and come with a seasoning packet for a soup base. They are also called ramen noodles.

Sashimi

Fresh, thinly sliced, uncooked salt water fish.

Sesame Oil

Sesame oil is the highly concentrated and very flavorful oil pressed from the sesame seed. It is especially prevalent in Korean and Chinese cooking.

321

Sesame Seeds

Aromatic white or black seeds often used in Asian cooking. May be purchased plain or roasted.

Shiitake Mushrooms

Shiitake mushrooms have brown or black caps from one to three inches in diameter. Although fresh shiitake mushrooms are available, the thick, dried mushrooms are far superior.

Shutome

A member of the billfish family, this fish is usually served pan fried. It is a white soft fleshed fish, up to 50 pounds. The meat is slightly oily and is mostly sold as steaks. Available during the spring.

Snow Peas

Also known as Chinese peas or sugar peas, snow peas are light green and crisp. The entire pod is edible and may be found frozen or fresh. To prepare, remove strings.

Soy Sauce

A liquid made of soy beans, barley and salt. Also known as shoyu.

Star Anise

A star-shaped dried spice with a delicate licorice flavor.

Star Fruit

Introduced to Hawai'i by the Chinese, this translucent yellow, waxy, star-shaped fruit possesses a delicate flavor. It is usually eaten fresh and cold, but may also be made into juice. The star fruit is mainly available during the winter months.

Tamari

Tamari is a rich, dark soy sauce that is brewed without wheat. It may be used as a dipping sauce, table condiment, or as a basting sauce.

Tarragon Vinegar

A vinegar, usually white wine vinegar, flavored with fresh tarragon.

Tofu

Tofu is a white bean curd or cake that has a custard-like consistency. It usually comes in blocks that are packed in water. Drain before using.

Uku

This gray snapper has mean-looking canine teeth and averages seven to eight pounds. It can reach up to fifty pounds.

Wasabi

A hot green horseradish powder used in Japanese cooking. To prepare the wasabi powder, mix with tepid water to form a thick paste. Let it sit for ten minutes to develop its flavor.

Water Chestnuts

These crispy white vegetables are covered with a thin, fine, brown-black skin. If fresh, pare before using. The canned variety is readily available.

Watercress

A green leafy plant that grows in shallow fresh running water. The leaves have a peppery flavor. Watercress is usually blanched or stir fried. The leaves and tender stems are used and the tough stems are discarded.

Wine Vinegar

This vinegar is made by fermenting white, red or rose wine. The type of wine will determine the flavor and color of the vinegar.

Won Bok

This tall, pale green celery cabbage is similar in appearance to romaine lettuce. It has a delicate, mild flavor and is also known as Chinese cabbage.

Anthuriums thrive in our tropical climate.
From the tiny red blossoms to the big, bold
green-and-white ones, the flowers are a favorite for
travelers to bring back from Hilo on the Big Island.

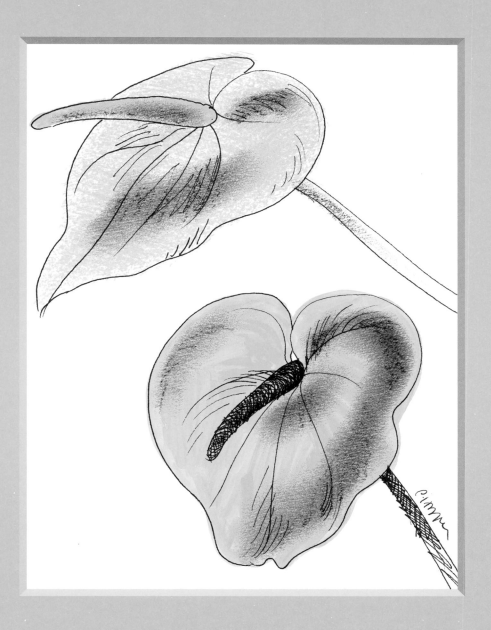

Index

a

Ahi

Aku

Almonds

Appetizers
Cold

Hot

Apples

Artichoke

Asparagus

A'u

Avocado

333

m

Macadamia Nuts
Biscotti **304**
Brownies Hawaiian Style **299**
Crustless Cranberry Pie **287**
Deluxe Carrot Cake **279**
Macadamia Nut Brittle **306**
Macadamia Nut Cheese Balls **21**
Macadamia Nut Pea Salad **57**
Macadamia Popcorn Crunch **307**
My Mom's Uncooked Fudge **305**
Super Lemon Bars **293**

Mango
Crunchy Baked Mangoes **261**
Mango Cream Cheese Pie **292**

Marinade
Bombay Chicken **128**
Cheri's Primo Shrimp **170**
Chicken Lychee **129**
Drunken Chicken Kabobs **137**
Grilled Marinated Leg of Lamb **177**
Hawaiian Barbequed Lamb **183**
Herb Marinated Shrimp **169**
Mary's Baby Lamb Chops **173**
Pacific Island Grill **176**
Papaya Curry Marinade **250**
Savory Lamb Kabobs **181**

Meatballs
Spaghetti Sauce with
    Turkey Meatballs **148**

Meats
(See Entrees)

Meringue
Almond Caramel Meringue **258**

Mexican
Chicken Soft Tacos **141**
Chilies Rellenos **189**
Jessica's Salsa **27**

Mexicali Eggplant **205**
Pali Picante Sauce **23**
Tijuana Torte **138**

Miso
Eggplant with Miso Sauce **217**

Mochiko
Baked Mochi **267**
Japanese Rice Crackers *(Arare)* **116**
Kascaran **264**
Mochiko Chicken Wings **145**

Mousse
Chocolate Mousse **259**

Muffins
Bran-ana Muffins **110**

Mushrooms
Chicken Assaggio **135**
Chicken with Herbs
    and Mushrooms **146**
Coquille Saint Jacques **172**
Cornish Hens with Wild Rice **131**
Drunken Chicken Kabobs **137**
Heavenly Shrimp **162**
Mushroom and Mozzarella
    Salad with Basil Dressing **59**
Mushroom Potato Frittata **232**
Pearl Barley Soup **98**
Sausalito Chicken **130**
Shrimp Bake **171**
Shrimp with Vegetables
    and Pasta **238**
Spaghetti Michi **237**
Tofu Tuna Bake **164**
Veal Marsala **184**
Wild Rice Casserole **227**

Mustard
Baked Chicken Dijon **152**
Bombay Chicken **128**
Glazed Curry Turkey **133**
Poulet Dijon **134**
Sance's Mustard Sauce **250**

Sauces

Appetizer
Jessica's Salsa **27**
Pali Picante Sauce **23**
Satay Sauce **247**
Dessert
Grandmother's Chocolate Sauce **260**
Luscious Lemon Sauce **269**
Onolicious Chocolate Sauce **260**
Main Dish
Aunty Olive's BBQ Sauce **248**
Chicken Siu Mai **150**
Ginger Beef with Raisin Sauce **182**
Haole Plum Sauce **245**
Marinara Sauce **186**
Oven-Barbecued Spareribs **180**
Sance's Mustard Sauce **250**
Satay Sauce **247**
Seared and Smoked Ahi with
   Pistachio Pesto, Ogo Wasabi Sauce
   and Radish Salsa **166**
Spaghetti Sauce with
   Turkey Meatballs **148**
Sweet and Sour Sauce for Fish **247**
Swordfish with Sweet and
   Sour Sauce **160**
Tangy Cucumber Sauce **249**
Zesty Cranberry Sauce **248**

Sausage

Julie's Rotini with Artichokes **235**
Sausage and Spinach Bake **236**
Sausage Minestrone **102**
Turkey Sausages **149**

Scallops

Coquille Saint Jacques **172**
Hawaiian Scallop Seviche **15**
Sunset Sea Scallops **168**

Seafood

(See Entrees)

Shallots

Dijon Tomato Fish Pouches **161**

Shellfish

(See individual listings, e.g.,
crab; fish; shrimp; etc.)

Sherry

Grilled Marinated Leg of Lamb **177**
Herb Marinated Shrimp **169**
Sherried Kula Onions **210**
Sherried Pumpkin Soup **95**

Shrimp

Avocado and Shrimp Salad **32**
Cheri's Primo Shrimp **170**
Chicken Siu Mai **150**
Hanauma Bay Pasta **226**
Heavenly Shrimp **162**
Herb Marinated Shrimp **169**
Lemon Marinated Shrimp **14**
Shrimp and Dill Sandwich **165**
Shrimp Artichoke Dip **24**
Shrimp Bake **171**
Shrimp Maunakea **18**
Shrimp Salad **70**
Shrimp Soup Orleans **99**
Shrimp with Lime-Soy Vinaigrette **63**
Shrimp with Vegetables and
   Pasta **238**

Shutome

Seared Shutome Medallions
   with Maui Onions and
   Kula Tomatoes **156**

Snow Peas

Cashew Pork **178**
Shrimp Maunakea **18**
Stuffed Snow Peas **34**

Sole

Sunset Seviche **28**

Sorbet

Papaya Sorbet **257**

Soufflé

Broccoli Soufflé **212**

The Committee

Davina Chun-Hom and Julie Ra-Goodman
Co-Chairpersons 1991-92

Gail Makinodan and Linda Naviaux
Co-Chairpersons 1992-93

Robbie Dingeman and Suzanne Peterson
Co-Chairpersons 1993-94

Tracy C. Jones
Editor

Kell Douglas
Recipe Coordinator

Anne Anderson
Art Director

Committee Members 1991-1993

Mary Mau
Erin Oshita Choy
Karen Ono
Mary Keller
Lissa Dunford
Kelly Cross
Chris Lau
Aileen Saito
Sherry Wilfong
Liz Grindle
Jean Hamakawa
Linda Martell
Alana Cline
Elizabeth Stillion
Beth Worrall-Daily
Jodi Maero
Deborah Lau Okamura
Gloria Morgan
Laurie Okamoto
Kathy Rueter
Debbie Wong
Rhonda Vadset
Paulette Yoshida
Marcia Warren

Experts

Dominique Jamain (Kahala Hilton)
Thomas Ky (Assaggio Italian Restaurant)
George Mavrothalassitis (Halekulani)
Gary Strehl (Hawaii Prince Hotel)
Pacific Broiler
Lois Taylor
Bess Press, Inc.

Advisor
Sally Mist (and honorary committee members:
Wakey, McKiven and Billy Mist)

345

Contributors

We acknowledge all of the individuals who contributed to the contents and production of this book, many of whom are listed here. Credit for this book goes to our many volunteers and friends who contributed their recipes, time, homes, special talents and ideas. We also wish to thank the women of the Junior League of Honolulu who made our first cookbook, *A Taste of Aloha*, a classic. We hope that *Another Taste of Aloha* will be as timeless.

Valerie Adams
Debbie Ahern
Shirlee Albrecht
Lucy Alexander
Amelia Andrade
Julie Ang
Cary Anzai
Amy Arapoff
Lynn Arimoto
Ann Armistead
Anne Asper-Davis
Alisa Au
Debby Atkinson
Cherie Axelrod
Martha Balkin
Helena Barahal
Carmen Basa
Mary Baumgardner
K.J. Bell
Margo Berg
Mary Begier
Mary Bershard
Valerie Blaisdell
Nancy Biller
Marita Collins Biven
Tess Blanco

Ann Botticelli
Bernice Bowers
Nancy Boyle
Kathy Brondes
Maureen Buckley
Sherri Bulkley
Lynne Bunch
Mary Burke
Beth Reaves Burroughs
Kathy Cabreros
Kimberly Caldwell
Phoebe Campbell
Merilyn Cannon
Christina Carlson
Connie Carr
Jane Carney
Sarah Casken
Fredrica Cassiday
Barbara Champion
Ellie Champion
Susie Childs
Sharon Ching
Cynthia Christensen
Kathy Christensen
Carl Choy
Liz Chun

Clayton Chun-Hom
Kathy Clifford
Terry Clifton
Janice Cole
Joanie Colman
Nancy Conley
Lore Cook
Jacqueline Corteway
Phyllis Corteway
Kathy Crandall
Heidi Cregor
Doris Crow
Patricia Culver
Diane Damon
Joan Danieley
Dottie Darrow
Dori Davis
Katie Desmarais
Gary Dias
Josephine B. Dingeman
Maria Di Tullio
Lindsay Dodge
Mary Jo Eline
Ann Fairfax Ellett
Jane Emerson-Brown
Krystal Emge

346

Wendy Farley
Pam Felix
Shelley Fernandez
Holly Fiocca
Susan Flowers
Julia Fong
Cynthia Fragale
C. R. Glenn
Laura Glenn
Jan Gordon
Beverley S. Grimmer
Judy Grimes
Randy Grobe
Anna Grune
Nancy Gurczyneski
Rhoda Hackler
Claire Hagenbuch
Lisa Hayashi
Carolyn Heitzman
Robin Park Helms
Lisa Hemmeter
Kim Hemmeter
Tina Henry
Mavis Higa
Sono Hirose-Hulbert
Nona Holmes
Missy Holmes
Kathy Hong
Tina Louise Hoogs
Catherine Howieson
Mina Humphreys
Debra Hunt
Mollie Hustace
Rona Ikehara
Dana Izumi
Krissy Izumi
Tracy Jaconette
Jackie Johnson

Lila Johnson
Claire Johnson
Stephanie Johnson
Jeffrie Jones
Susan Kamida
Mary Ann Kelly
Paula Kelly
Doug Kilpatrick
Karen Kimbrell
Adrienne King
Julie King
Ann Klaug
Dale Klein
Dawn Krause
Laura Konda
Diane Kudo
Elizabeth Lacy
Lyn Lam
Amy Lamparello
Elizabeth B. Lee
Lennie Lee
Sherree Lee
Susan Leong
Melissa Lewis
Amy Li
Robin Liu
Georgia Locks
John Locks
Ben Locquiao
Shannon Lowrey
Joseph Lovell
Ann Lozada
Rita Luppino
Kimberly Luyckx
Victoria Lyman
Andrea Lyon
Helen MacNeil
Dorothy Manly

Barbara Marumoto
Kim Marumoto
Susu Markham
Mary Marx
Betty Mastrantonio
Lenora Matsuda
Nancy Maxwell
Wendy Maxwell
Amy Mc Cormack
Lieala McCullen
Teresa McDonald
Madeleine McKay
Vera McKenzie
Kay McWayne
Nancy Meguro
Laura Mellow
P. Merillat
Pat Metcalf
Naomi Mihara
Gerry Milnor
Lisa Moore
Susan Moore
Susan Morrill
Julie Ann Morris
Shannon Morrison
DeEtte Mountford
Margo Mun
Lisa Munger
Myrna Murdoch
Jessica Myrabo
Cindy Nichols
Maggie O'Brien
Suzanne and Warren
   O'Donell
Carolyn O'Keefe
Hae Okimoto
Cary Olin
Nancy O'Malley

Maile Ostrem
Carol Lee Owens
Sandy Pablo
Nancy Pace
Sybil Padgett
Lou Parsons
Shelley Pasko
Barbara Petrus
Barbara Phillips
Beryl Pierce
Kathy Prenger
Darnney Proudfoot
Melissa Goldsmith
    Pryor
Eileen Quinn
Lori Rand
Susan Rehberg-Merrill
Donna Reid-Hayes
Allene Richardson
Pokey Richardson
Debbie Robertson
Lori Roberts-Mitchell
Ellen Roos-Marr
Cathy Rungee
Kathy Sabota
Aileen Saito
Mary Saunders
Lissa Schiff
Lori Schlueter
Cynthia Schnack

Mari-Jo Schull
Laurel Schuster
Menakoki Schwan
Julie B. Schwarz
Val Schweigert
Tina Semenza
Monica Shaney
Sharon Shanley
Pat Shimizu
Lisa Siegfried
Sara Silverman
Cheryl Sisler
Julie Sloane
Celeste Smith
Diana Snyder
Katy Soldner
Irish Sonnenberg
Susan Soong
Karen Sotomura
Aileen Stephanos
Nancy Stephenson
Peggy Stitham
Karen Sumner
Anne Swank
Betty Swindle
Diana Snyder
Corinne Takasaki
Cynthia Thielen
Nicki Thompson
Penelope Thune

Lynne Tokumaru
Gay Tsukamaki
Mindy Tucker
Karen Turran
June Udell
Carol Vieira
Marcia Warren
Jojo Watumull
Mary Wessberg
Lael Wheeler
Theresa Whitaker
Tookie White
Kari Wilhite
Elizabeth Wiser
Susan Witten
Cynthia Wo
Paulette Wo
Cyndi Wright Wong
Sandy Wong
Vicki Woolford
Karen Wright
Linda Wright Wong
Leslie Wynhoff
Ruthann Yamanaka
Debbie Yee
Andrea Yip
Annie Yonashiro
Paulette Yoshida
Patti Young
Debra Yuen

Mahalo for your support.
Proceeds from Another Taste of Aloha
are reinvested back into the community
through projects, programs, volunteer training and grants.
Our current and past projects include:

Kindergarten Nutrition Work • The Place
Follow Up Clinic, Queen's Hospital • Mental Health Association
Social Service Committee • Kula Kokua Therapeutic Pre-School
Follow the Leader Conference • Artmobile
Volunteer in Probation (VIP Slide Show) • Volunteers for Deaf and Blind
Supplied Books to American Merchant Marine Association
Sponsorship Concerts • Waikiki Aquarium • Children's Theater
Hawaii Bound School • Palama Settlement—Auditorium Equipment
The Family in Hawaii Conference • Family Health Leaning Center
Occupational Therapist, Queen's Hospital • Historic Hawaii Foundation
Boards of Public Parks &Recreation
White House Conference on Families (State Coordinator)
Mental Hygiene Society of Hawaii • Kids in the Courts
Oahu Health Council—Exhibits • Volunteer Leadership Program
Volunteer Service Bureau • Palama Settlement—Instructor
Human Service TV • Hawaii Nature Center
Rehabilitation Center—Swimming Pool • H.U.G. (Helping Us Grow)
Hawaii children's Museum of Art, Science & Technology
TV for Rehabilitation Center • Action Line
HCT Children's Summer Director • Honolulu Theatre for Youth
Hospital Pavilion (State Hospital) • Bishop Museum Observatory
Turnaround–A Play for Parents • Keiki Concerts
Hale Kipa–Independent Living Program
Hawaii Special Olympics • Primary and Intermediate Concerts
Prevent Elder Abuse • Juvenile Detention Home
Teen Pregnancy Intervention Program (Association Set-Up)
White House Conference on Children and Youth
Honolulu Academy of Arts–Gifted Child Studios
Enhancements, Children's Advocacy Center
Waimano Home–Equipment and Volunteers
Library of Hawaii–Books & Story Telling • Iolani Palace Restoration
Historic Task Force–TV Programs and Pamphlets
Zoo Education Program • Preschool Pet Education (PET)
Air & Water Pollution Conference • Foundation Friends
Pohukaina School–Equipment and Volunteers
Shelters for Abused Spouses and Children • AIDS Education
Na Ki'i Na Na 'Opio • My Bag • The Learning Years
Christmas in April Oahu
Independent Living • Learning Years
The Family Violence Prevention Program • Hey Coach
The Family Visitation Center • Blueprint for Change
Ke Kulana Wahine, The YWCA of Oahu Women's Resource Center

About the Artist

Pegge Hopper has lived in Hawaii since 1963. She was born in Oakland, California and studied at the Art Center College of Design in Pasadena, California.

Pegge's first job was in New York City with Raymond Loewy designing murals for department stores. This was followed by a year of traveling throughout Europe and ultimately working as a designer in Milan, Italy for La Rinascente, a large chain of department stores. Pegge feels that the experience she gained in Europe has been a major influence in her work.

She has had her own gallery in the Chinatown section of Honolulu since 1983, where her original paintings, drawings, and collages, as well as posters and limited edition prints are available. Pegge has had one-person shows in Chicago, Los Angeles, Seattle, and in Hawaii at the Contemporary Arts Center. Her work is represented in many private and public collections including the permanent collections of the Hawaii State Foundation on Culture and the Arts, The Honolulu Advertiser and Contemporary Arts Center in Hawaii, the Dai Ichi Hotel in Tokyo, the Ala Moana Hotel in Honolulu, American Hawaii Cruise Lines, and the Bishop Museum.

Another Taste of Aloha

The Perfect Gift

Share the gift of Aloha

Please send _____ ***Another Taste of Aloha*** cookbook(s)
@ $24.95 each (hardcover) .... _____

Please send _____ The original ***Taste of Aloha*** cookbook(s)
@ $24.95 each (hardcover) .... _____
(prices include postage & handling)
Total enclosed _____

No C.O.D., no foreign checks or currency. Please make checks payable to:
JLH Commercial Publications
Please allow 4-6 weeks for delivery.
Express delivery available on request.

_____ Payment Enclosed

_____ Please charge my ____VISA ____ MasterCard.

Name: _____

Account #: _____ Exp. Date: _____

Telephone, day: ( ) _____ evening: ( ) _____

Signature _____

Send to:
Name: _____

Address: _____

City: _____ State: _____ Zip: _____

Mail or fax this form to:
JUNIOR LEAGUE OF HONOLULU
Commercial Publications Office
1050 Ala Moana Blvd., Bldg. A, Bay 1, Honolulu, HI 96814
Fax: (808) 596-0206   Phone: (808) 596-2006

Ask us about other gift ideas.

Prices are subject to change without notice.

Thank you for your support.
*Proceeds from **Another Taste of Aloha** will be returned to the community*
through projects sponsored by the Junior League of Honolulu.